THE GUITALELE®
CHORD BIBLE
(ADGCEA Standard Tuning)

by

Tobe A. Richards

A Fretted Friends Publication for Cabot Books

Published by:
Cabot Books
Copyright © 2017 by Cabot Books
All rights reserved.

First Edition January 2017

ISBN-13: 978-1-912087-63-1

Cabot Books
3 Kenton Mews
Henleaze
Bristol
BS9 4LT
United Kingdom

Visit our online site at www.frettedfriendsmusic.com
e-mail: cabotbooks@blueyonder.co.uk

Guitalele® is a registered trade mark of Yamaha Corporation 2013.

TABLE OF CONTENTS

INTRODUCTION

The Guitalele Chord Bible provides the musician with 1,728 chords in all keys, featuring 68 different chord types, with 3 variations of each standard chord. 144 major slash chords are also included, together with 48 moveable chord shape diagrams (providing access to a further 576 barré and standard moveable chords) making this the most comprehensive reference guide for the guitalele currently available. For many years now, guitarists have been able to pick up a songbook and instantly play the songs in front of them, either with the help of one of the many published guides, or through the chord boxes supplied with most popular music. With the help of this *Chord Bible*, beginners and experienced guitalele players alike will be able to take advantage of the many songbooks, fake books and musical compendiums by any artist you would care to name, from *The Beatles* to *Joan Baez*, from *Planxty* to *The Pogues* or *Springsteen* to *Simon & Garfunkel*. With 68 different chordal variations in all keys, virtually any song should be playable!

Having a good chordal knowledge should arguably be the bedrock in any fretted or keyboard musicians armoury. Whether you're playing rock, pop, folk, jazz, blues, country or other types of music, it's impossible to supply a suitable accompaniment to any vocal or solo instrumental music without providing a chordal or harmonic backing. The subtle nuance of an added ninth chord over a major chord is something that can't be captured simply by playing a melody line. In theory it is possible to approximate the harmonic intervals of any music using a limited palette of chords - probably around ten to twelve. But wherever possible it's best to use correct harmonies if they're available to you.

Having six strings, the guitalele is a versatile instrument, making a wide variety of harmonic variations readily available. Despite this, sometimes compromises have to be made, particularly when a chordal configuration isn't available. But by making acceptable compromises and omitting the least important parts of that chord, even the most complex musical structures are then viable. For instance, in the case of an eleventh, the third is generally omitted without the character of the chord being adversely affected. Equally, the root or key note isn't always necessary to achieve an effective approximation of the full chord. The third is rarely missing from the majority of chords (other than elevenths) as it determines whether the key is major or minor - although this isn't a hard and fast rule, particularly in folk music where the root and fifth form the basis of most traditional music. These two intervals are generally the starting point for a number of open tunings of instruments as diverse as the guitar, the Irish bouzouki and the mountain dulcimer. The same interval is also used in a lot of heavy rock where a fifth chord is described as a *power chord*. Even though a power chord is technically neither major nor minor, it's more often used as an alternative for a major chord in most popular music.

One question which often pops up is *how many chords do I need to learn?* The smart answer is *'how long is a piece of string?'*, which is true, but it doesn't actually answer the question if you don't know where to start. My advice would be to begin with simple chord clusters like the popular G, C, D and Em progression and gradually work in new ones as you advance. If you intend playing within a rock format, it's probably sensible to learn the E, A, B sequence which is the staple of most guitarists and bassists. As a generalisation, jazz probably requires the greatest chordal knowledge of any form of music, so the learning curve will be longer if you're planning to pick up any songbook and instantly produce a recognisable version of your favourite *Duke Ellington* or *Steely Dan* number. The only truth as far as harmonic knowledge goes is you can never learn *too* much!

In this series of chord theory books, I've included a comprehensive selection of configurations of chords in all keys. As I mentioned previously, this will enable you to pick up virtually any songbook or fake book (topline melody and chord symbols) and look up the chord shape that's needed. Obviously, you'll come across the occasional song which doesn't conform to the normal harmonic intervals which you find in this, or any other chord theory publication, but with a little experimentation and experience, you'll be able to make a reasonable stab at it. For instance, most players would be more than a little bemused if they sud-

4

denly came across an instruction to play a *Gbmaj7add6/D*. Fortunately, this is fairly unusual, but from the knowledge you'll have learned, you'll be able to use a similar chord or work it out note by note. Put simply, if *every* theoretically possible chord shape were to be included in this or any other book, the result would resemble something akin to several volumes of the *Yellow Pages*!

FINGERING

Always a tricky subject and one which seems to generate a lot of discussion and differing opinions as to which method is correct. Personally, I take the view that it's a largely fruitless exercise, as the number of variables involved make a definitive answer unlikely. So what I've decided to do in this book is to choose fingering positions which feel comfortable to me. Some chord shapes will dictate the fingering used, but others will be down to personal preference. If you can practise your two and three finger chords using different fingers, it will make your playing a lot more fluid when you change to another chord shape. But if you develop habits which limit you to one playing position, it isn't the end of the world either, if you can make the transitions seamless.

The only rules, if you could loosely call them that, are:-

a) Don't abandon using your pinky or little finger if you're just beginning to play, as you'll eventually need it for some of the four finger chords which frequently crop up.

b) Try to avoid fretting with the thumb unless you're learning an instrument like the mountain dulcimer which requires a longer stretch. I know a number of players employ it on slimmer necked instruments, but I personally feel it leads to bad habits.

c) Keep your left hand fingernails short or fretting becomes a major problem. Obviously do the reverse if you're a lefty.

d) If you're a beginner and you're naturally left handed, don't get persuaded into buying a right handed instrument - it won't work! The learning curve will be steeper and you'll never get the fluidity you'd achieve with your natural hand. Most acoustic instruments can be adapted for a left hander apart from cutaway guitars and f-style mandolins etc., by reversing the nut and strings. For the non-reversible instruments, always go for a left handed model.

e) Learn to barré with other fingers apart from your index finger. This will prove invaluable with more complex chords and increase finger strength as well.

f) Don't be afraid to use fingerings further up the neck in combination with open strings as these will give you interesting new voicings and are generally quite popular in folk music. A number of these are provided in this book.

g) The guitalele should generally be played with the fingers, rather than a pick or plectrum, because the nylon strings would wear out very quickly.

CHORD THEORY & FAQs

Q *What is a chord?*

A It's a collection of three or more notes played simultaneously. The exceptions in this book are the fourths and fifths (power chords) which aren't in the strictest sense, true chords. For convenience sake, they are classed as such.

Q *What is a triad?*

A A chord containing three notes. For example, G Major, Bm, D+ or Asus4.

Q *What are intervals?*

A Intervals are the musical distance between notes in a musical scale. For instance in the scale of C Major, C is the 1st note, D is the 2nd note, E the 3rd and so on. So if you're playing the chord of C Major, your intervals will be 1–3–5 or C as the *first* note, E as the *third* note and G as the *perfect fifth*.

Q *What is a chromatic scale and which intervals does it contain?*

A: A chromatic scale encompasses all twelve notes in a musical scale, including the sharps and flats. It's also the basis for the naming of *every* chord in existence. See the staff diagram below to see the intervals:

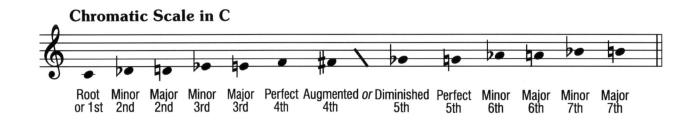

Q *What is a seventh chord?*

A: In its most basic form, an additional note beyond the triad. Sevenths can be either major or flattened. For instance, returning to our old friend, the key of C, a *Cmaj7* has an added *B* on top of the *C–E–G* triad. The resultant chord has a mellow quality often found in jazz. Now if you take the B and flatten it by dropping the fourth note in your chord down to a B flat, you get a C7.

Q: *Then why isn't it called a C minor seventh?*

A: Technically this *is* a minor seventh note, but this would create a lot of confusion when naming chords, as you already have a minor interval option in your triad (in the key of C major, E flat), so it's always referred to as a 7th to differentiate between it and a major seventh.

Q: *What is an extension?*

A: A chord which goes beyond the scope of triads and sevenths. Basically, extensions are additional notes placed above the triad or seventh in a musical stave, fingerboard or keyboard. It's important to understand these are, for theoretical purposes, always placed above the seventh. Or in layman's terms, higher up the scale. The confusion comes when you start to realise a 9th is identical to a 2nd - in the scale of C – a D note.

Q: *So why is the ninth note the same as the second note?*

A: This takes a little grasping, but if you remember that if your note goes higher than the seventh it's a 9th, but if it's lower, it'll be a 2nd. An example of this would be Csus2, which contains the root note of C, a 2nd or suspended D note and a G, the perfect 5th. You'll see this even more clearly if you look at the piano keyboard diagram below. Count from the C up to the following D beyond the 7th (B note). From the C to the second D is exactly nine whole notes.

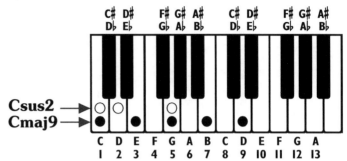

Q: *Do any other extensions share a common note?*

A: Yes, other examples include the *11th*, which is also a *4th* and the *13th* which shares a note with the *6th*.

Q: *What are inversions?*

A: In the root version of a chord, the notes run in their correct order from lowest to highest. In the case of G major, it would be G–B–D. With an inversion of the same chord the notes would run in a different order. For example, the first inversion of G major would be B–D–G and the second, D–G–B. In general, triads sound more or less the same when they're inverted, but that's certainly not the case with sevenths and extensions which can sound quite different and occasionally discordant when the notes are jumbled up in certain configurations. Inversions can also produce different chords using the same basic notes. A good example of this would be *C6 (C-E-G-A)* which produces an *Am7 (A-C-E-G)* when it's inverted (both contain the notes of C–E–G–A, but in a different order). The major variations are in the tonal properties of the chords, making them sound quite different from one another.

Q: *Do elevenths and thirteenths have any particular properties?*

A: Yes. In most cases the 3rd is omitted from eleventh chords and the 11th from the majority of thirteenths as they're deemed unnecessary and arguably, create unwanted dissonance.

Q: *Some chords are called by different names in different music books. What should I do?*

A: The alternative chord name reference chart at the back of the book should help sort out the confusion.

Q: *What is a suspended chord?*

A: It's simpler to think of suspended chords as a stepping stone to a major or resolving chord. In effect the third has been left in a state of suspension by either raising it to a fourth (sus4) or lowering it to a second (sus2). Sevenths also provide versions of the suspended chord in the form of C7sus4 or C7sus2 (using the key of C as an example).

Q: *What is a diminished chord?*

A: A diminished chord has a dissonent quality to it where the third and fifth notes in a triad are flattened by a semi-tone. Again, using C as an example, C major (C-E-G) is altered to Cdim (C-E♭-G♭). A second version of a dimished chord is also used in many forms of music, the diminished seventh. This retains the elements of a standard diminished chord, adding a double flat in the seventh (C-E♭-G♭-B♭♭). A B♭♭ in this case is, to all intents and purposes, really an A note.

Q: *What is an augmented chord?*

A: An augmented chord basically performs the opposite task to a diminished one. Instead of lowering the fifth by a semitone, it raises it by the same interval. A C+ (augmented) chord contains the triad of C-E-G♯. The major root and third are retained and the fifth is sharpened.

UNDERSTANDING THE CHORD BOXES

The three diagrams below show the chord conventions illustrated in this guide. Most experienced fretted instrument players should be familiar with them. The suggested fingering positions are only meant as a general guide and will depend, in many instances, on hand size, finger length and flexibility, so feel free to experiment. The location of the black circles is unalterable, though, if you want to produce the correct voicing.

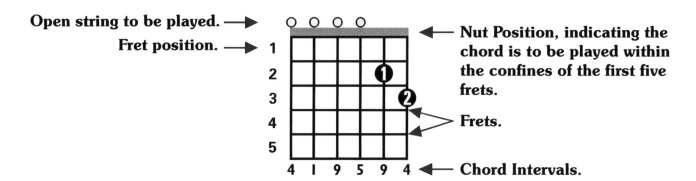

Open string to be played. →
Fret position. →

← Nut Position, indicating the chord is to be played within the confines of the first five frets.

Frets.

← Chord Intervals.

If there are no markers above or below the string, the string should not be played.

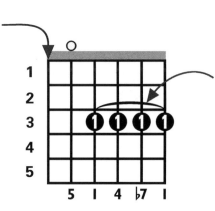

Barré chord (in this example, a four string barré to be fretted with the index finger).

Suggested fingering. In this case the 1st or index finger marker is displayed.

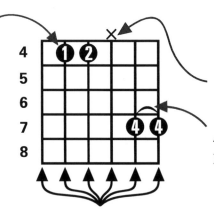

A damped string. In this example the 3rd string should be damped using the lower pad of the middle finger, fretting the 4th string.

A two string barré to be played with the fourth finger.

Left to right: 6th, 5th, 4th, 3rd, 2nd and 1st courses of strings.

Whether a fretted instrument has single strings or pairs of strings, the chord boxes in this book, other chord dictionaries and songbooks treat it as a four stringed instrument. This convention is common to all double or triple course instruments such as the mandolin or tiple, making the diagrams a lot less confusing and free from unnecessary clutter.

GUITALELE
FINGERBOARD & TUNING LAYOUT

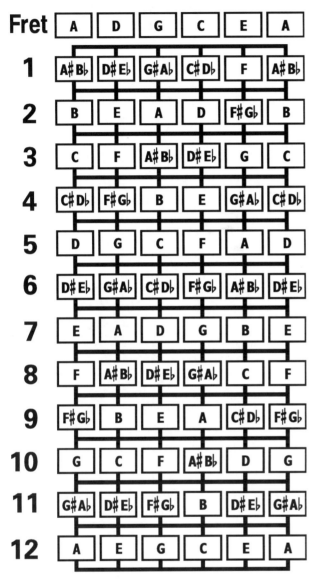

Fingerboard note layout

Guitalele tuning features the same note configuration as capoing a guitar on the 5th fret.

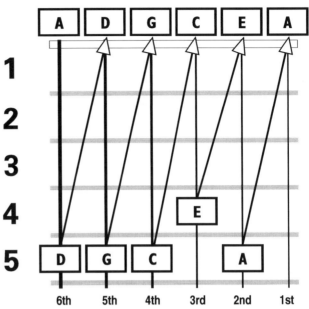

Tuning the guitalele by fretting at given intervals on the fingerboard.

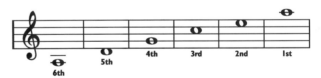

Guitalele tuning in written notation (top) and true pitch (bottom). The guitalele uses standard guitar notation even though it's tuned a 4th higher.

To tune your guitalele accurately, it's best to use an electronic chromatic tuner, but if there isn't one available, you can tune it to a guitar or piano/electronic keyboard. The following tuning grid gives the correct fingering positions on the guitar fingerboard and piano keyboard.

Guitalele	Guitar	Piano
1st string (A)	1st string (E) fretted at the 5th fret	1st A above middle C
2nd string (E)	1st open string (E)	1st E above middle C
3rd string (C)	2nd string (B) fretted at the 1st fret	Middle C
4th string (G)	3rd open string (G)	1st G below middle C
5th string (D)	4th open string (D)	1st D above middle C
6th string (A)	5th open string (A)	2nd A below middle C

THE CHORDS COVERED IN THIS BOOK

Chord	Chord Name in Full	Harmonic Interval
C	Major	1–3–5
Cm	Minor	1–F3-5
C-5	Major Diminished Fifth	1–3–F5
C°	Diminished	1–F3—F5
C4	Fourth	1–4
C5	Fifth or Power Chord	1–5
Csus2	Suspended Second	1–2–5
Csus4	Suspended Fourth	1–4–5
Csus4add9	Suspended Fourth Added Ninth	1–4–5–9
C+	Augmented	1–3–S5
C6	Major Sixth	1–3–5–6
Cadd9	Major Added Ninth	1–3–5–9
Cadd11	Major Added Eleventh	1–3–5–11
Cm6	Minor Sixth	1–F3–5–6
Cm-6	Minor Diminished Sixth	1–F3–5–F6
Cmadd9	Minor Added Ninth	1–F3–5–9
C6add9	Major Sixth Added Ninth	1–3–5–6–9
Cm6add9	Minor Sixth Added Ninth	1–F3–5–6–9
C°7	Diminished Seventh	1–F3–F5–DF7
C7	Seventh	1–3–5–F7
C7sus2	Seventh Suspended Second	1–2–5–F7
C7sus4	Seventh Suspended Fourth	1–4–5–F7
C7-5	Seventh Diminished Fifth	1–3–F5–F7
C7+5	Seventh Augmented Fifth	1–3–S5–F7
C7-9	Seventh Minor Ninth	1–3–5–F7–F9
C7+9	Seventh Augmented Ninth	1–3–5–F7–S9
C7-5-9	Seventh Diminished Fifth Minor Ninth	1–3–F5–F7–F9
C7-5+9	Seventh Diminished Fifth Augmented Ninth	1–3–F5–F7–S9
C7+5-9	Seventh Augmented Fifth Minor Ninth	1–3–S5–F7–F9
C7+5+9	Seventh Augmented Fifth Augmented Ninth	1–3–S5–F7–S9
C7add11	Seventh Added Eleventh	1–3–5–F7–11
C7+11	Seventh Augmented Eleventh	1–3–5–F7–S11
C7add13	Seventh Added Thirteenth	1–3–5–F7–13
Cm7	Minor Seventh	1–F3–5–F7
Cm7-5	Minor Seventh Diminished Fifth	1–F3–F5–F7
Cm7-5-9	Minor Seventh Diminished Fifth Minor Ninth	1–F3–F5–F7–F9
Cm7-9	Minor Seventh Minor Ninth	1–F3–5–F7–F9
Cm7add11	Minor Seventh Added Eleventh	1–F3–5–F7–11
Cm(maj7)	Minor Major Seventh	1–F3–5–7
Cmaj7	Major Seventh	1–3–5–7
Cmaj7-5	Major Seventh Diminished Fifth	1–3–F5–7
Cmaj7+5	Major Seventh Augmented Fifth	1–3–S5–7
Cmaj7+11	Major Seventh Augmented Eleventh	1–3–5–7–S11
C9	Ninth	1–3–5–F7–9
C9sus4	Ninth Suspended Fourth	1–4–5–F7–9
C9-5	Ninth Diminished Fifth	1–3–F5–F7–9
C9+5	Ninth Augmented Fifth	1–3–S5–F7–9
C9+11	Ninth Augmented Eleventh	1–3–5–F7–9–S11
Cm9	Minor Ninth	1–F3–5–F7–9

Chord	Chord Name in Full	Harmonic Interval
Cm9-5	Minor Ninth Diminished Fifth	1–F3–F5–F7–9
Cm(maj9)	Minor Major Ninth	1–F3–5–7–9
Cmaj9	Major Ninth	1–3–5–7–9
Cmaj9-5	Major Ninth Diminished Fifth	1–3–F5–7–9
Cmaj9+5	Major Ninth Augmented Fifth	1–3–S5–7–9
Cmaj9add6	Major Ninth Added Sixth	1–3–5–6–7–9
Cmaj9+11	Major Ninth Augmented Eleventh	1–3–5–7–9–S11
C11	Eleventh	1–3–5–F7–9–11
C11-9	Eleventh Diminished Ninth	1–3–5–F7–F9–11
Cm11	Minor Eleventh	1–F3–5–F7–9–11
Cmaj11	Major Eleventh	1–3–5–7–9–11
C13	Thirteenth	1–3–5–F7–9–11–13
C13sus4	Thirteenth Suspended Fourth	1–4–5–F7–9–11–13
C13-5-9	Thirteenth Diminished Fifth Minor Ninth	1–3–F5–F7–F9–11–13
C13-9	Thirteenth Minor Ninth	1–3–5–F7–F9–11–13
C13+9	Thirteenth Augmented Ninth	1–3–5–F7–S9–11–13
C13+11	Thirteenth Augmented Eleventh	1–3–5–F7–9–S11–13
Cm13	Minor Thirteenth	1–F3–5–F7–9–11–13
Cmaj13	Major Thirteenth	1–3–5–7–9–11–13

Key: F = Flat   S = Sharp   DF = Double Flat

SLASH CHORDS

What is a slash chord? Put simply, they're standard chords with an added note in the bass. *So what differentiates a C chord from a C/G when the G is already part of that chord, in this case, the fifth?* Theoretically, nothing, but the difference is very apparent when you actually sound the chord. The G bass is emphasised to provide a different feel to the harmonics. Slashes are also commonly found when the music calls for a descending bassline. For example; C, C/B, C/A and C/G.

The note after the slash indicates the bass note being played. For instance D/B would be an instruction to play a D chord with a B bass.

Slash Note. Generally found on the 6th & 5th or 4th strings.

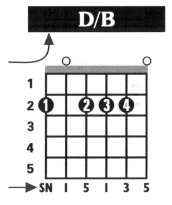

How do I play a slash chord that isn't listed in this book? Well, firstly, it would be an almost impossible task to cover every possible slash chord in existence, because the variations are potentially even greater than with standard chords. What you can do, within the confines of this guide, is to find the part of the chord before the slash in the main body of the book and then look for the nearest bass note on the fifth or sixth strings. To find the right bass note, consult the fingerboard layout on *page 9*.

USING A CAPO (OR *CAPO D'ASTRA*)

Using a capo is a quick and easy way of changing key to suit a different vocal range or to join in with with other musicians playing in a different key. For the uniniated, a capo is a moveable bar that clamps onto the fingerboard of fretted instruments. It works in much the same way as using a finger barré to hold down the strings. They come in a variety of designs and prices, the simplest using a metal rod covered in rubber and sprung with elastic. For the guitalele, look for a standard guitar capo.

C Chords

C
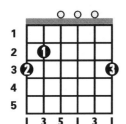
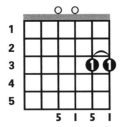
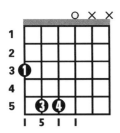

Cm
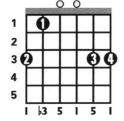
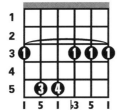
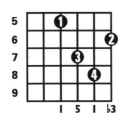

C7
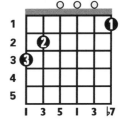
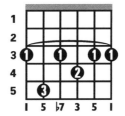
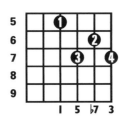

Cm7
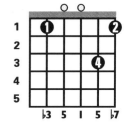
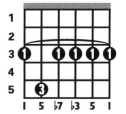
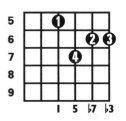

C5
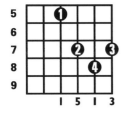
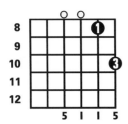

C6
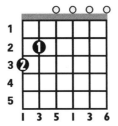
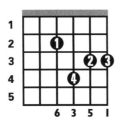
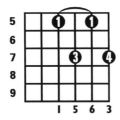

Cm6
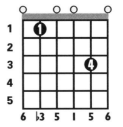
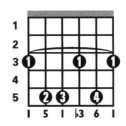
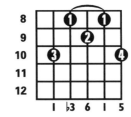

Cmaj7
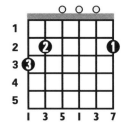
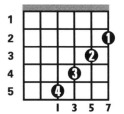
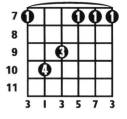

C Chords

C°
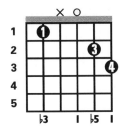
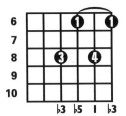
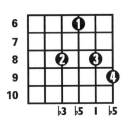

C°7
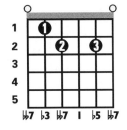
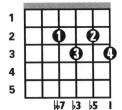
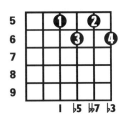

C-5
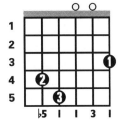
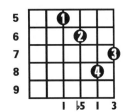
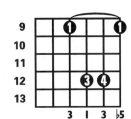

C+
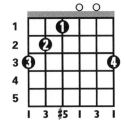
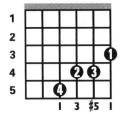
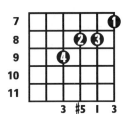

Csus2
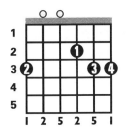
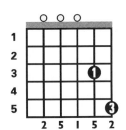
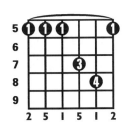

Csus4
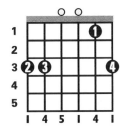
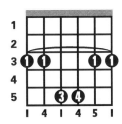
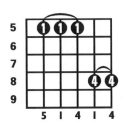

C7sus4
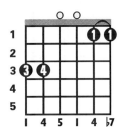
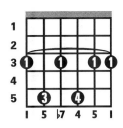
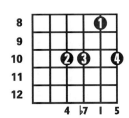

Cm7-5
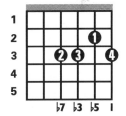
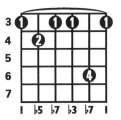
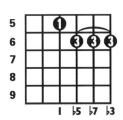

C Chords

Cadd9
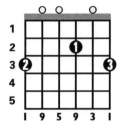
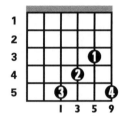
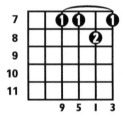

Cmadd9
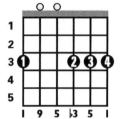
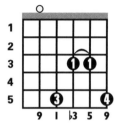
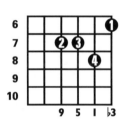

C6add9
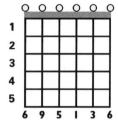
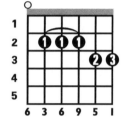
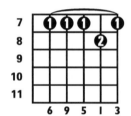

Cm6add9
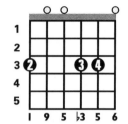
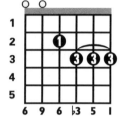
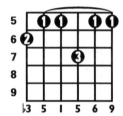

C7-5
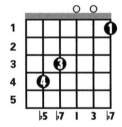
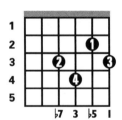
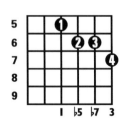

C7+5
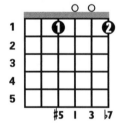
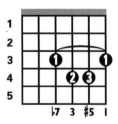
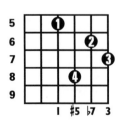

C7-9
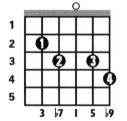
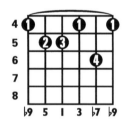
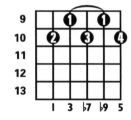

C7+9
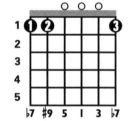
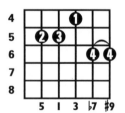
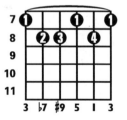

Cm(maj7)

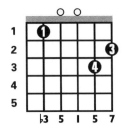

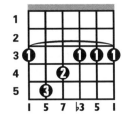

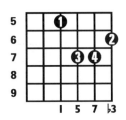

Cmaj7-5

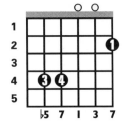

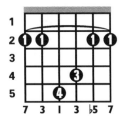

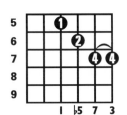

Cmaj7+5

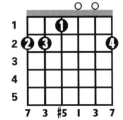

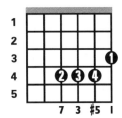

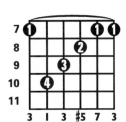

C9

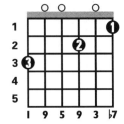

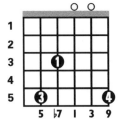

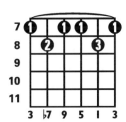

Cm9

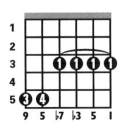

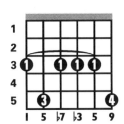

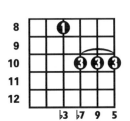

Cmaj9

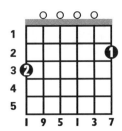

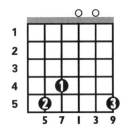

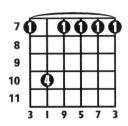

C11

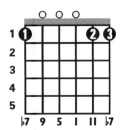

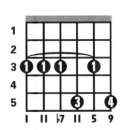

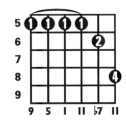

C13

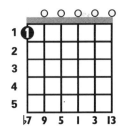

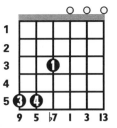

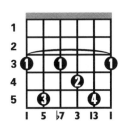

C Chords (Advanced)

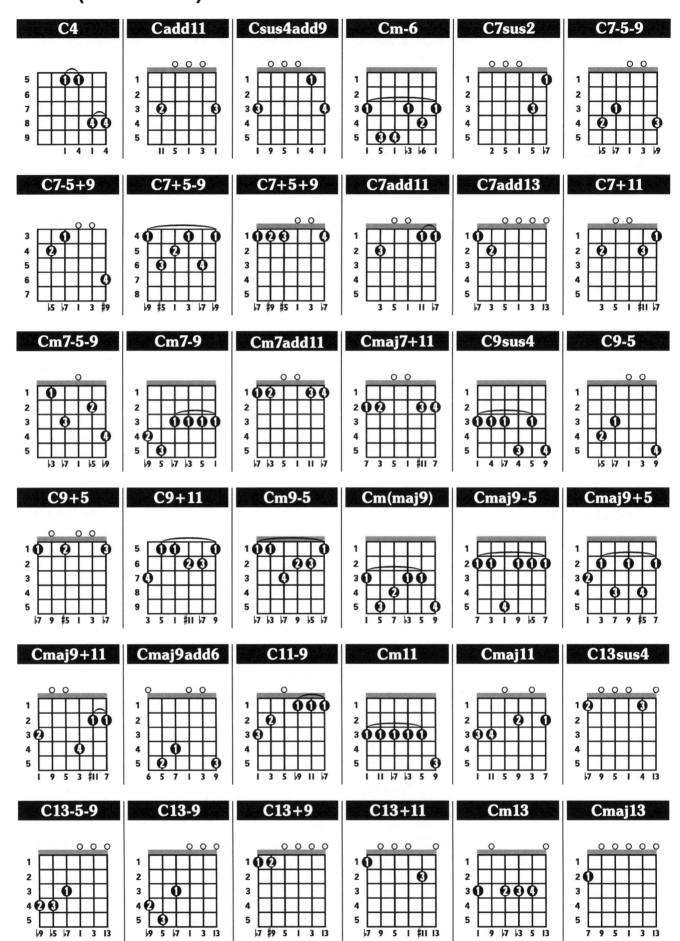

Db
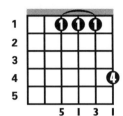
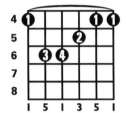
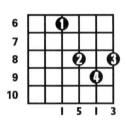

Dbm
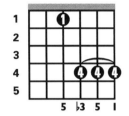
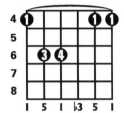
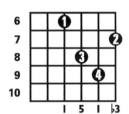

Db7
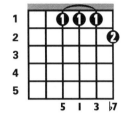
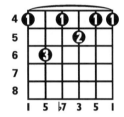
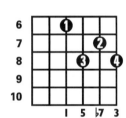

Dbm7
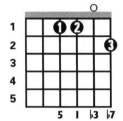
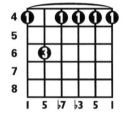
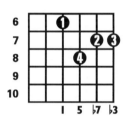

Db5
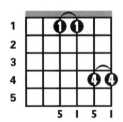
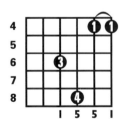
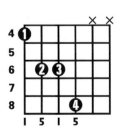

Db6
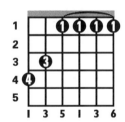
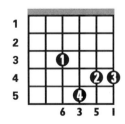
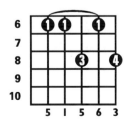

Dbm6
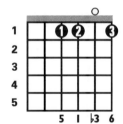
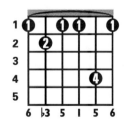
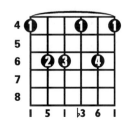

Dbmaj7
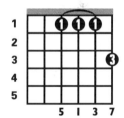
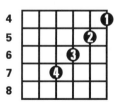
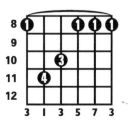

C# / D♭ Chords

D♭°
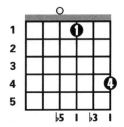
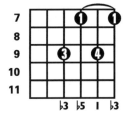
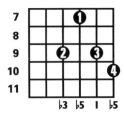

D♭°7
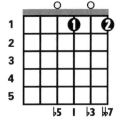
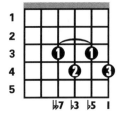
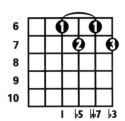

D♭-5
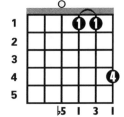
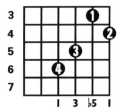
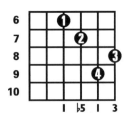

D♭+
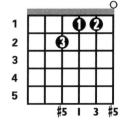
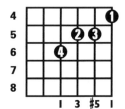
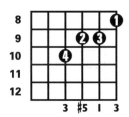

D♭sus2
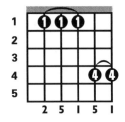
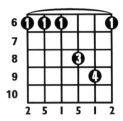
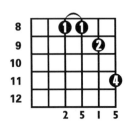

D♭sus4
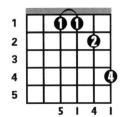
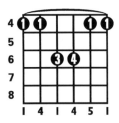
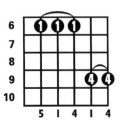

D♭7sus4
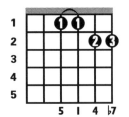
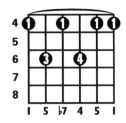
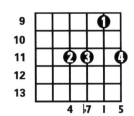

D♭m7-5
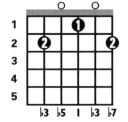
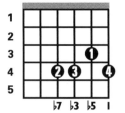
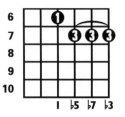

D♭add9

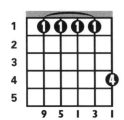

9 5 1 3 1

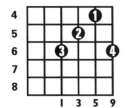

1 3 5 9

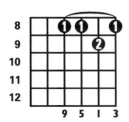

9 5 1 3

D♭madd9

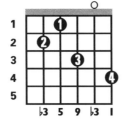

♭3 5 9 ♭3 1

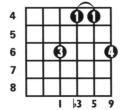

1 ♭3 5 9

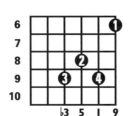

♭3 5 1 9

D♭6add9

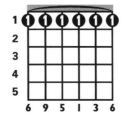

6 9 5 1 3 6

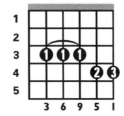

3 6 9 5 1

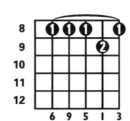

6 9 5 1 3

D♭m6add9

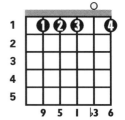

9 5 1 ♭3 6

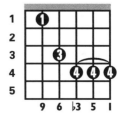

9 6 ♭3 5 1

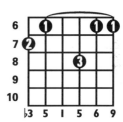

♭3 5 1 5 6 9

D♭7-5

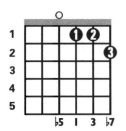

♭5 1 3 ♭7

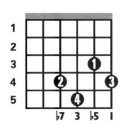

♭7 3 ♭5 1

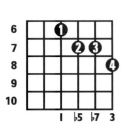

1 ♭5 ♭7 3

D♭7+5

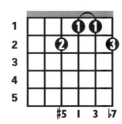

#5 1 3 ♭7

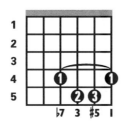

♭7 3 #5 1

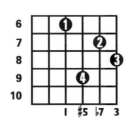

1 #5 ♭7 3

D♭7-9

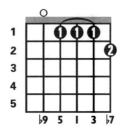

♭9 5 1 3 ♭7

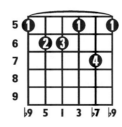

♭9 5 1 3 ♭7 ♭9

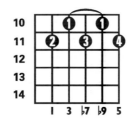

1 3 ♭7 ♭9 5

D♭7+9

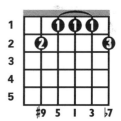

#9 5 1 3 ♭7

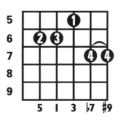

5 1 3 ♭7 #9

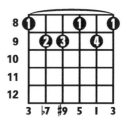

3 ♭7 #9 5 1 3

19

C#/ D♭ Chords

D♭m(maj7)

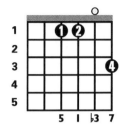

5   1   ♭3   7

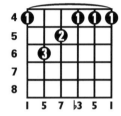

1   5   7   ♭3   5   1

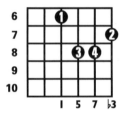

1   5   7   ♭3

D♭maj7-5

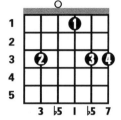

3   ♭5   1   ♭5   7

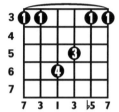

7   3   1   3   ♭5   7

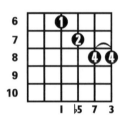

1   ♭5   7   3

D♭maj7+5

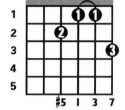

#5   1   3   7

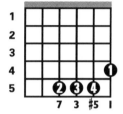

7   3   #5   1

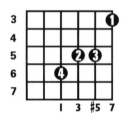

1   3   #5   7

D♭9

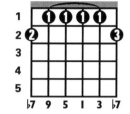

♭7   9   5   1   3   ♭7

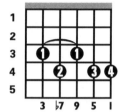

3   ♭7   9   5   1

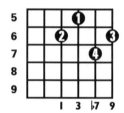

1   3   ♭7   9

D♭m9

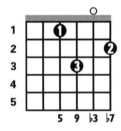

5   9   ♭3   ♭7

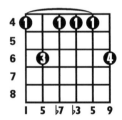

1   5   ♭7   ♭3   5   9

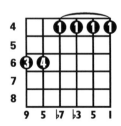

9   5   ♭7   ♭3   5   1

D♭maj9

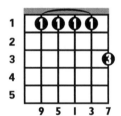

9   5   1   3   7

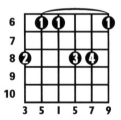

3   5   1   5   7   9

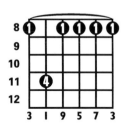

3   1   9   5   7   3

D♭11

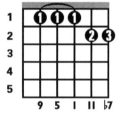

9   5   1   11   ♭7

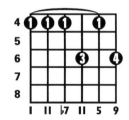

1   11   ♭7   11   5   9

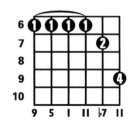

9   5   1   11   ♭7   11

D♭13

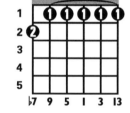

♭7   9   5   1   3   13

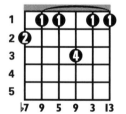

♭7   9   5   9   3   13

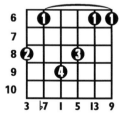

3   ♭7   1   5   13   9

20

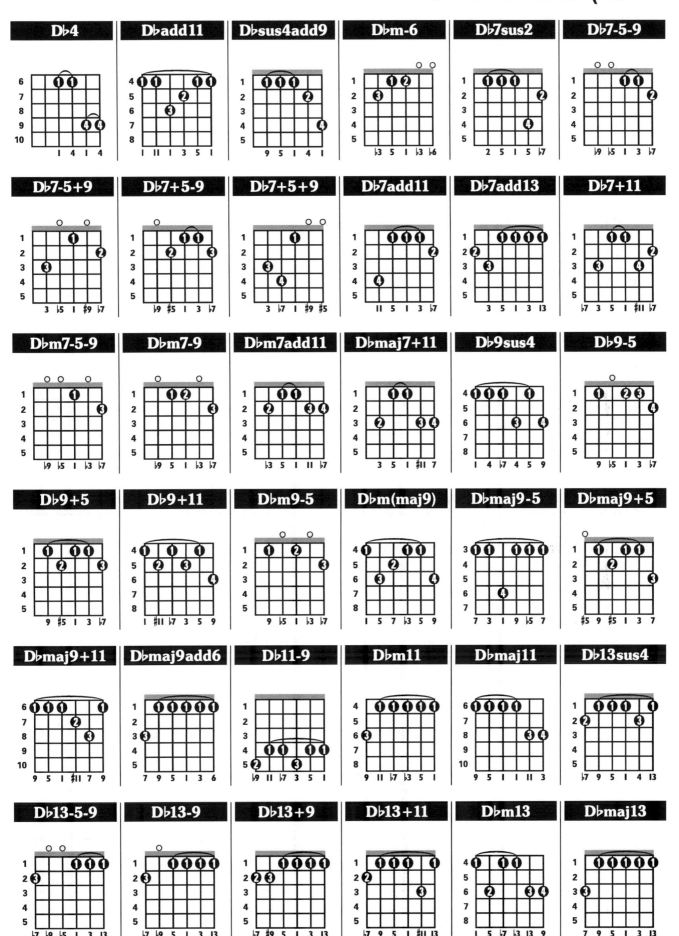

D Chords

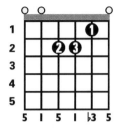
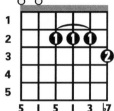
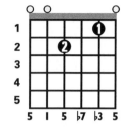

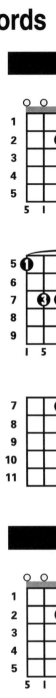
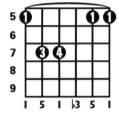

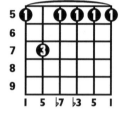

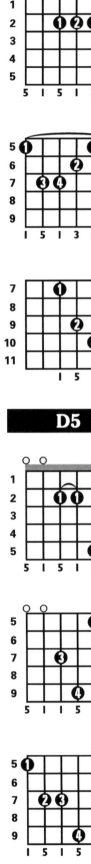
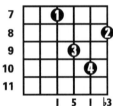
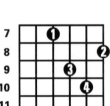
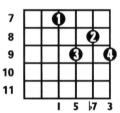
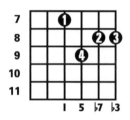

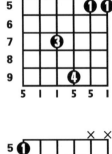
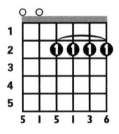
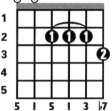
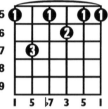
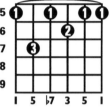
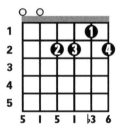
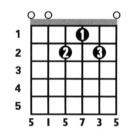

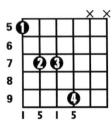
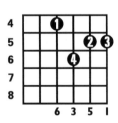
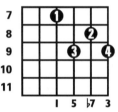
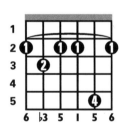
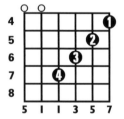

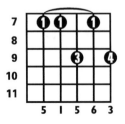
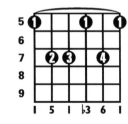
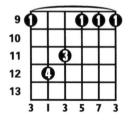

D°
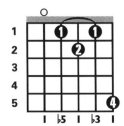
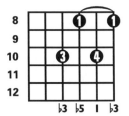
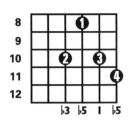

D°7
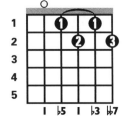
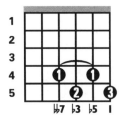
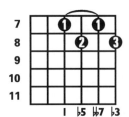

D-5
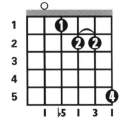
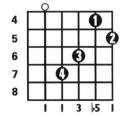
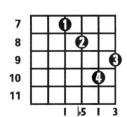

D+
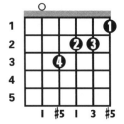
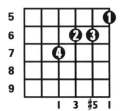
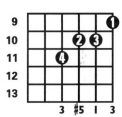

Dsus2
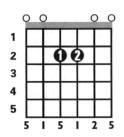
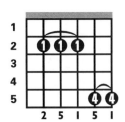
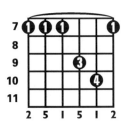

Dsus4
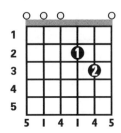
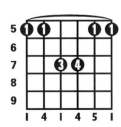
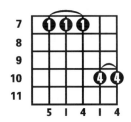

D7sus4
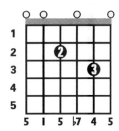
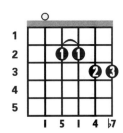
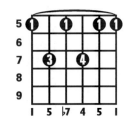

Dm7-5
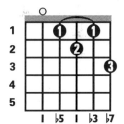
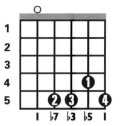
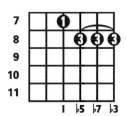

D Chords

Dadd9	Dmadd9	D6add9	Dm6add9
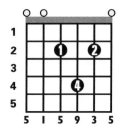	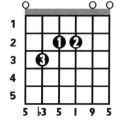	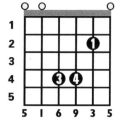	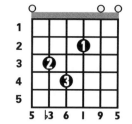
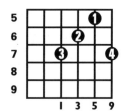	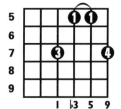	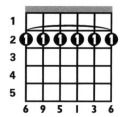	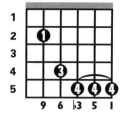
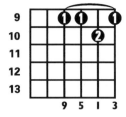	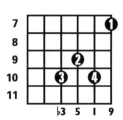	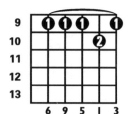	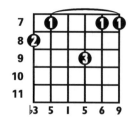

D7-5	D7+5	D7-9	D7+9
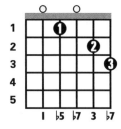	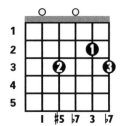	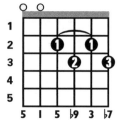	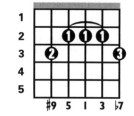
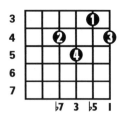	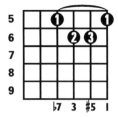	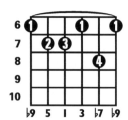	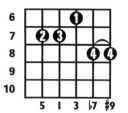
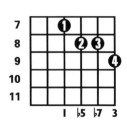	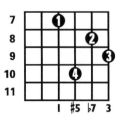	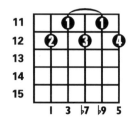	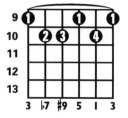

24

Dm(maj7)

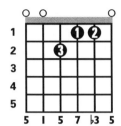
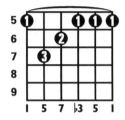
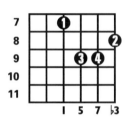

Dmaj7-5

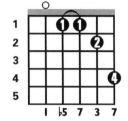
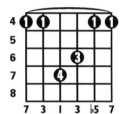
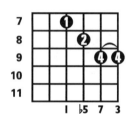

Dmaj7+5

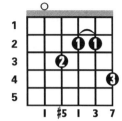
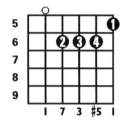
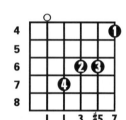

D9

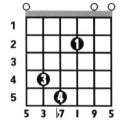
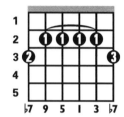
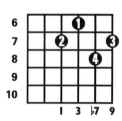

Dm9

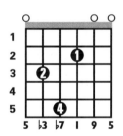
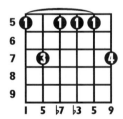
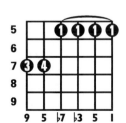

Dmaj9

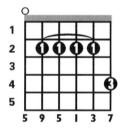
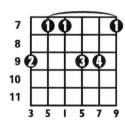
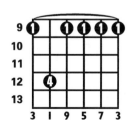

D11

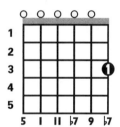
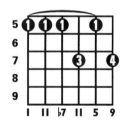
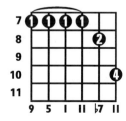

D13

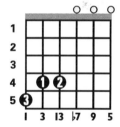
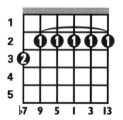
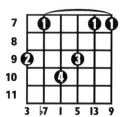

D Chords (Advanced)

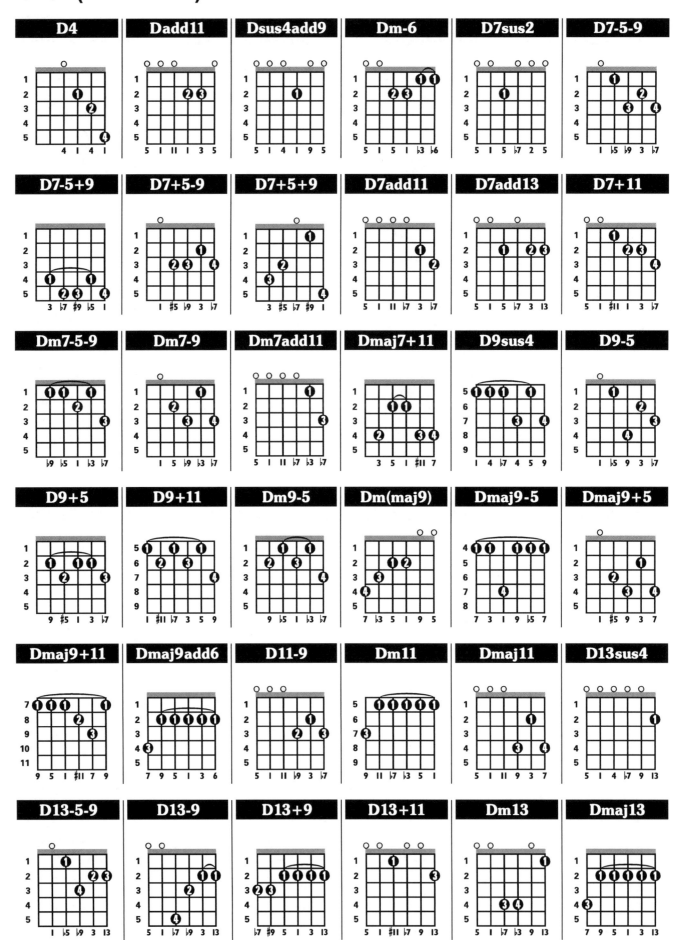

E♭

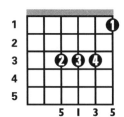

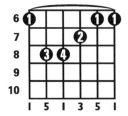

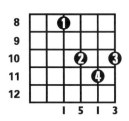

E♭m

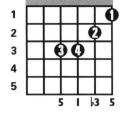

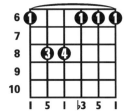

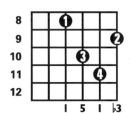

E♭7

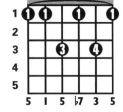

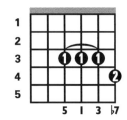

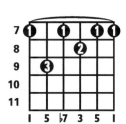

E♭m7

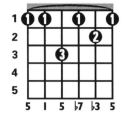

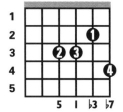

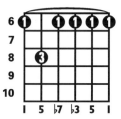

E♭5

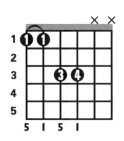

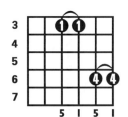

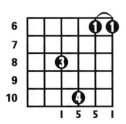

E♭6

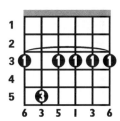

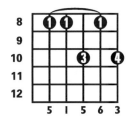

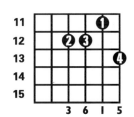

E♭m6

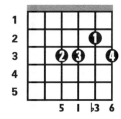

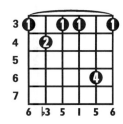

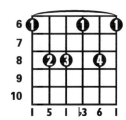

E♭maj7

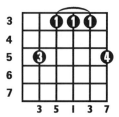

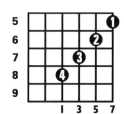

D#/ E♭ Chords

E♭°	E♭°7	E♭-5	E♭+

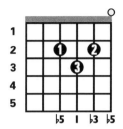 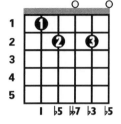 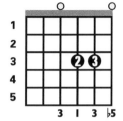 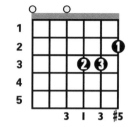

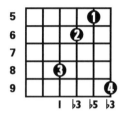 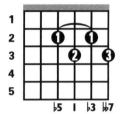 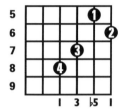 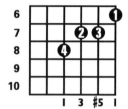

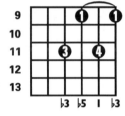 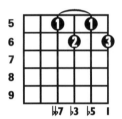 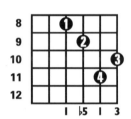 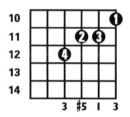

E♭sus2	E♭sus4	E♭7sus4	E♭m7-5

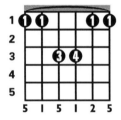 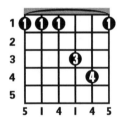 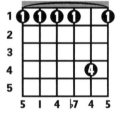 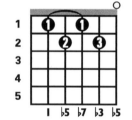

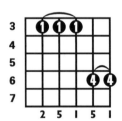 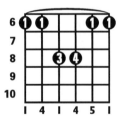 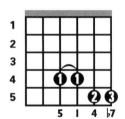 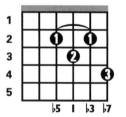

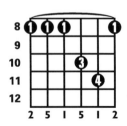 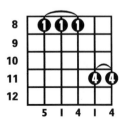 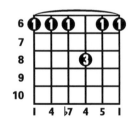 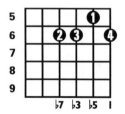

E♭add9
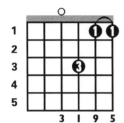
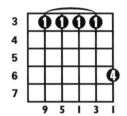
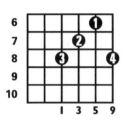

E♭madd9
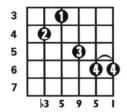
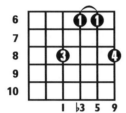
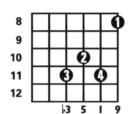

E♭6add9
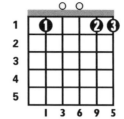
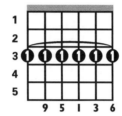
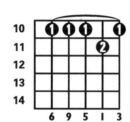

E♭m6add9
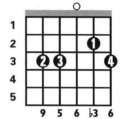
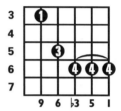
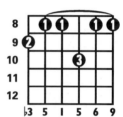

E♭7-5
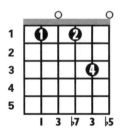
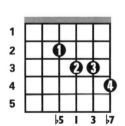
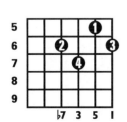

E♭7+5
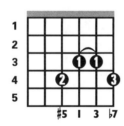
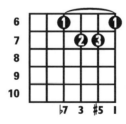
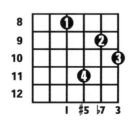

E♭7-9
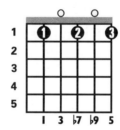
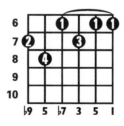
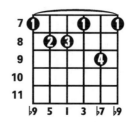

E♭7+9
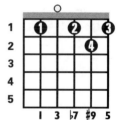
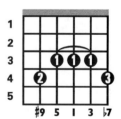
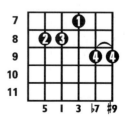

29

D#/ E♭ Chords

E♭m(maj7)

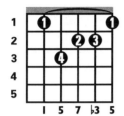

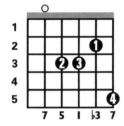

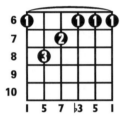

E♭maj7-5

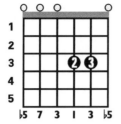

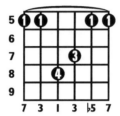

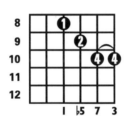

E♭maj7+5

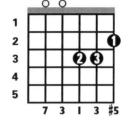

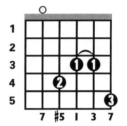

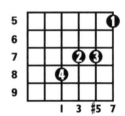

E♭9

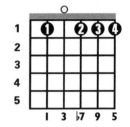

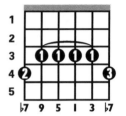

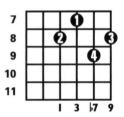

E♭m9

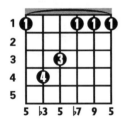

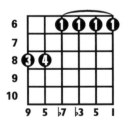

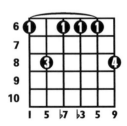

E♭maj9

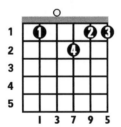

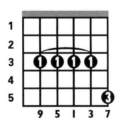

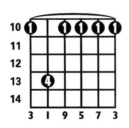

E♭11

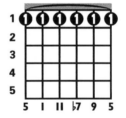

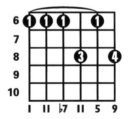

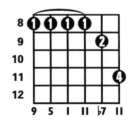

E♭13

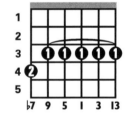

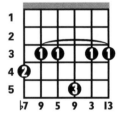

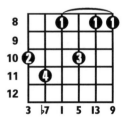

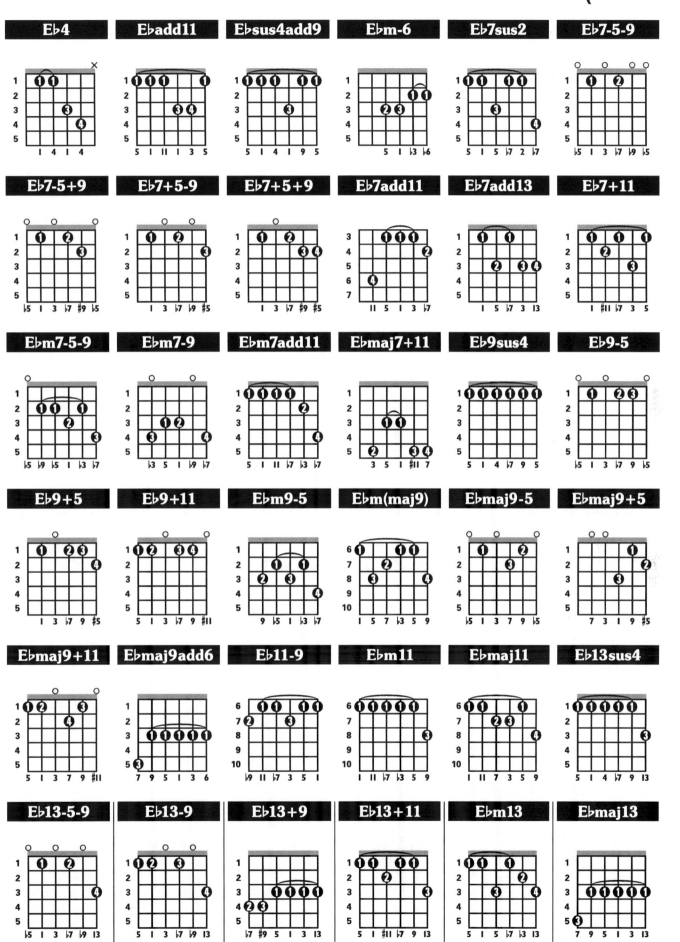

E Chords

E	Em	E7	Em7
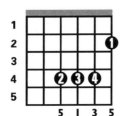	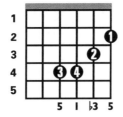	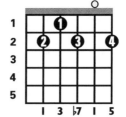	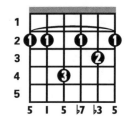
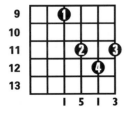	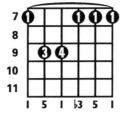	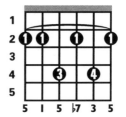	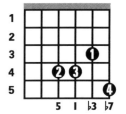
	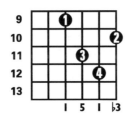	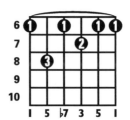	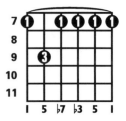

E5	E6	Em6	Emaj7
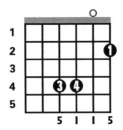	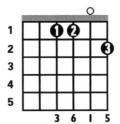	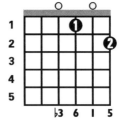	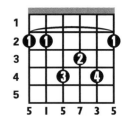
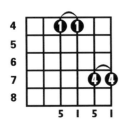	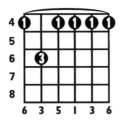	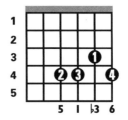	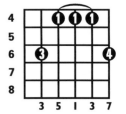
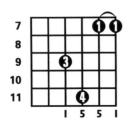	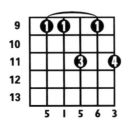	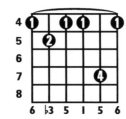	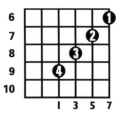

E°

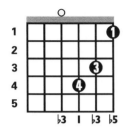

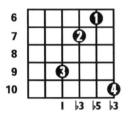

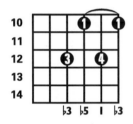

E°7

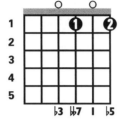

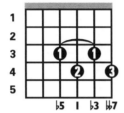

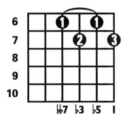

E-5

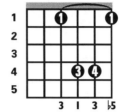

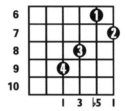

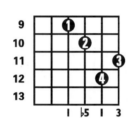

E+

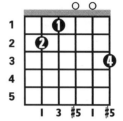

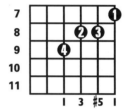

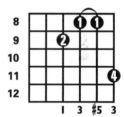

Esus2

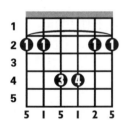

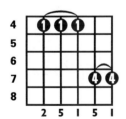

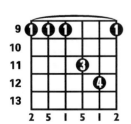

Esus4

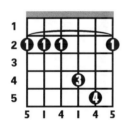

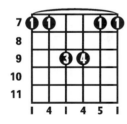

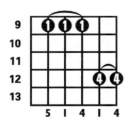

E7sus4

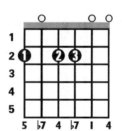

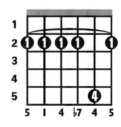

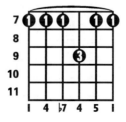

Em7-5

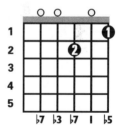

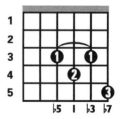

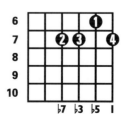

E Chords

Eadd9

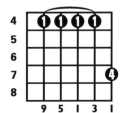

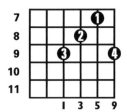

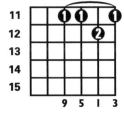

Emadd9

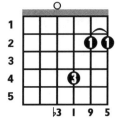

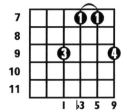

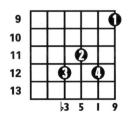

E6add9

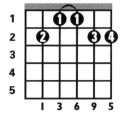

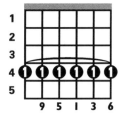

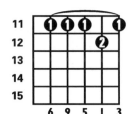

Em6add9

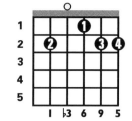

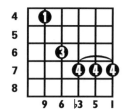

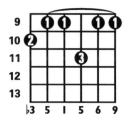

E7-5

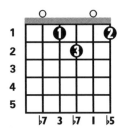

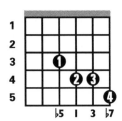

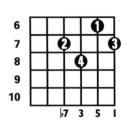

E7+5

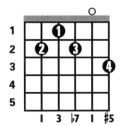

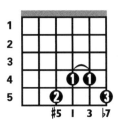

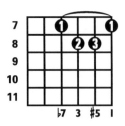

E7-9

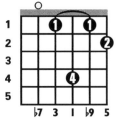

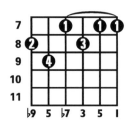

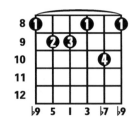

E7+9

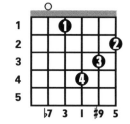

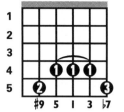

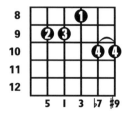

Em(maj7)

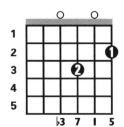

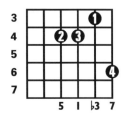

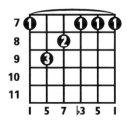

Emaj7-5

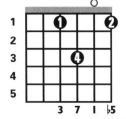

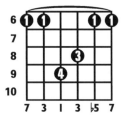

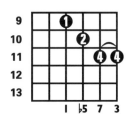

Emaj7+5

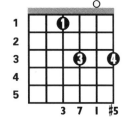

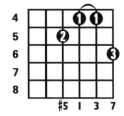

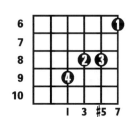

E9

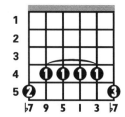

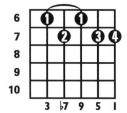

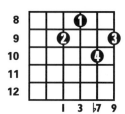

Em9

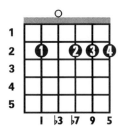

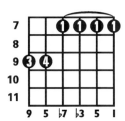

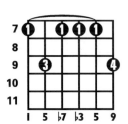

Emaj9

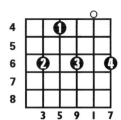

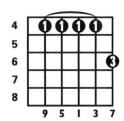

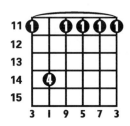

E11

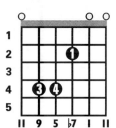

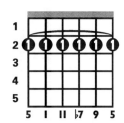

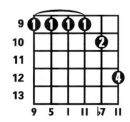

E13

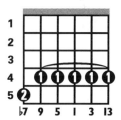

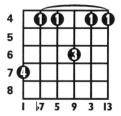

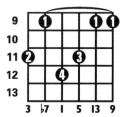

E Chords (Advanced)

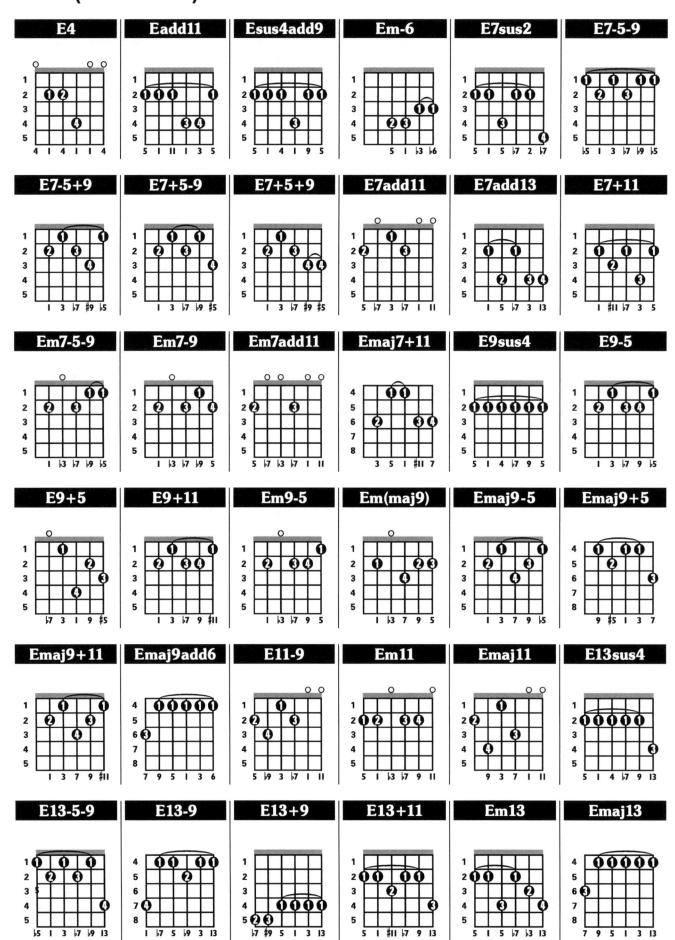

F Chords

F

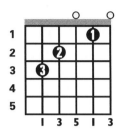

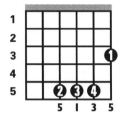

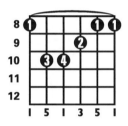

Fm

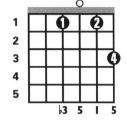

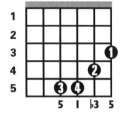

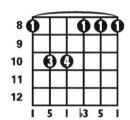

F7

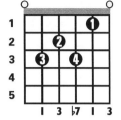

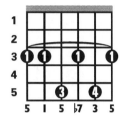

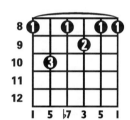

Fm7

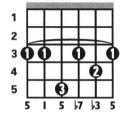

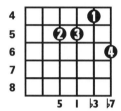

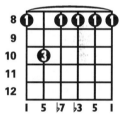

F5

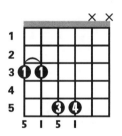

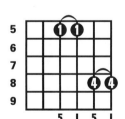

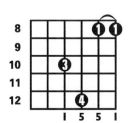

F6

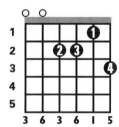

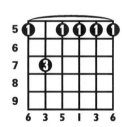

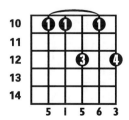

Fm6

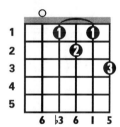

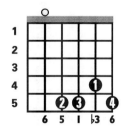

Fmaj7

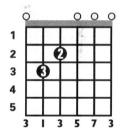

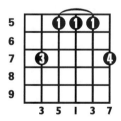

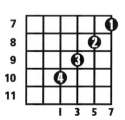

F Chords

F°
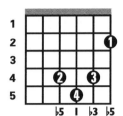
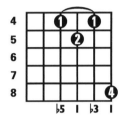
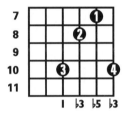

F°7
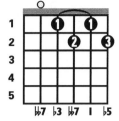
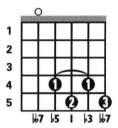
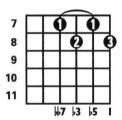

F-5
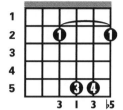
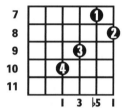
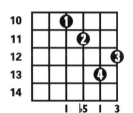

F+
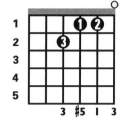
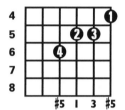
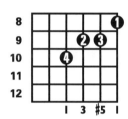

Fsus2
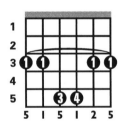
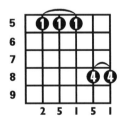
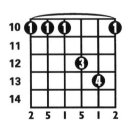

Fsus4
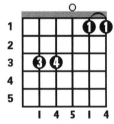
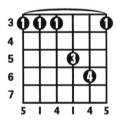
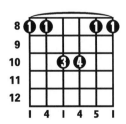

F7sus4
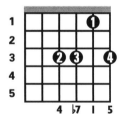
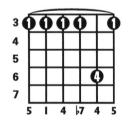
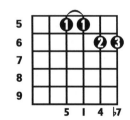

Fm7-5
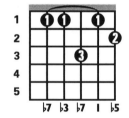
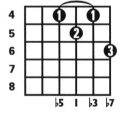
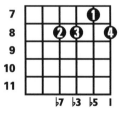

Fadd9
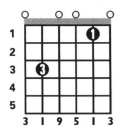
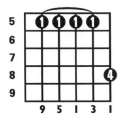
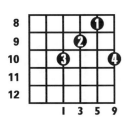

Fmadd9
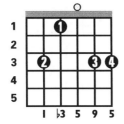
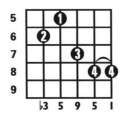
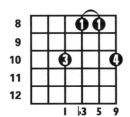

F6add9
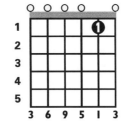
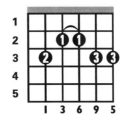
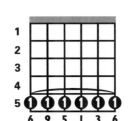

Fm6add9
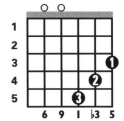
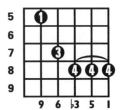
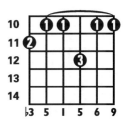

F7-5
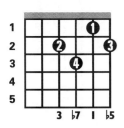
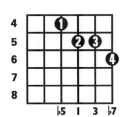
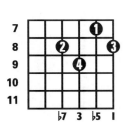

F7+5
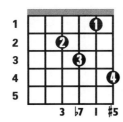
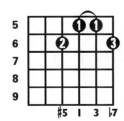
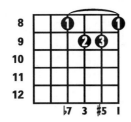

F7-9
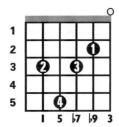
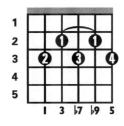
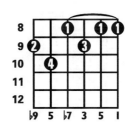

F7+9
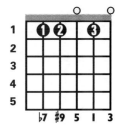
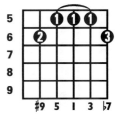
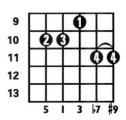

F Chords

Fm(maj7)
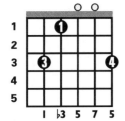
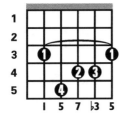
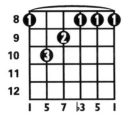

Fmaj7-5
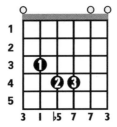
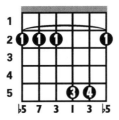
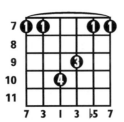

Fmaj7+5
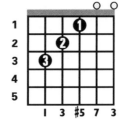
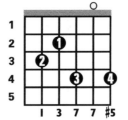
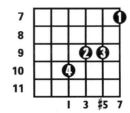

F9
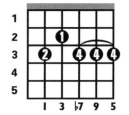
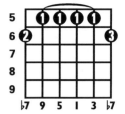
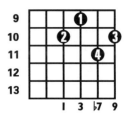

Fm9
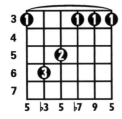
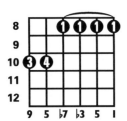
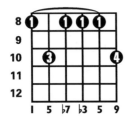

Fmaj9
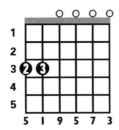
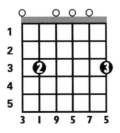
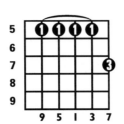

F11
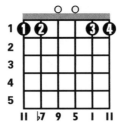
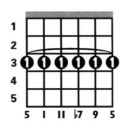
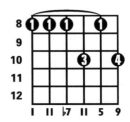

F13
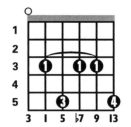
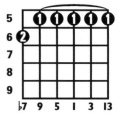
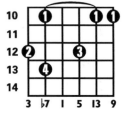

40

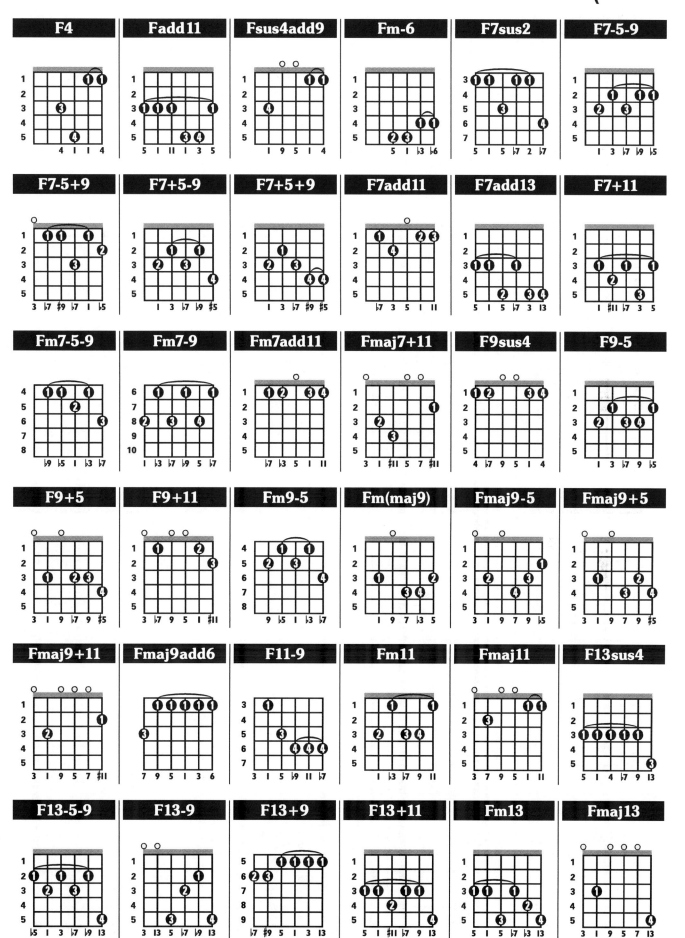

F♯/ G♭ Chords

F#	F#m	F#7	F#m7

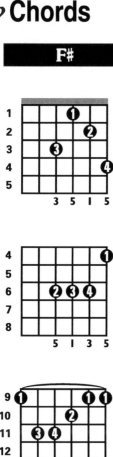 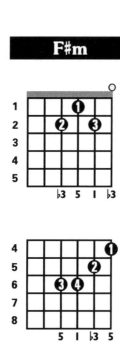 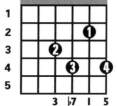 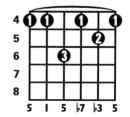

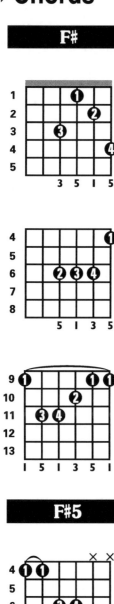 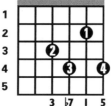 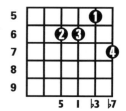

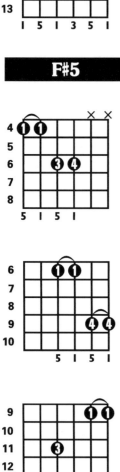 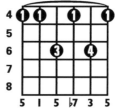 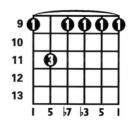

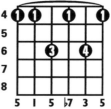

F#5	F#6	F#m6	F#maj7

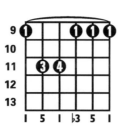 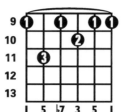 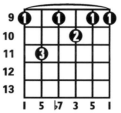 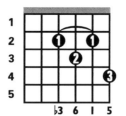

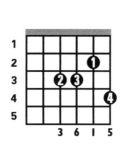 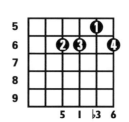 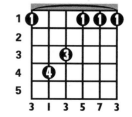

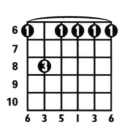 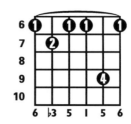 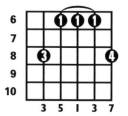

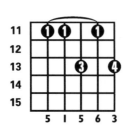 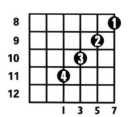

F#°

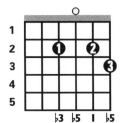

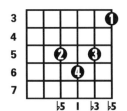

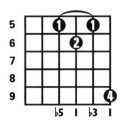

F#°7

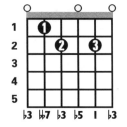

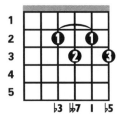

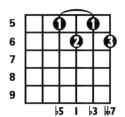

F#-5

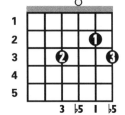

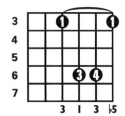

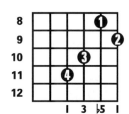

F#+

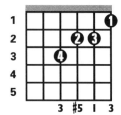

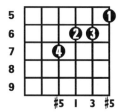

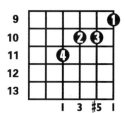

F#sus2

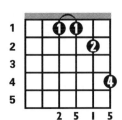

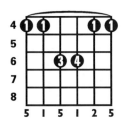

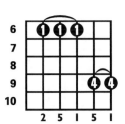

F#sus4

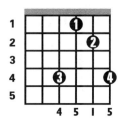

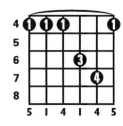

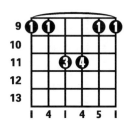

F#7sus4

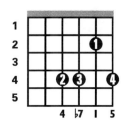

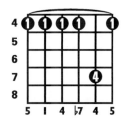

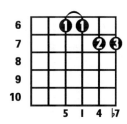

F#m7-5

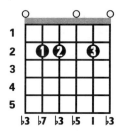

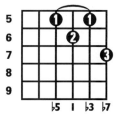

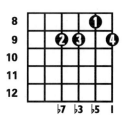

F#/ G♭ Chords

F#add9
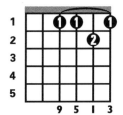
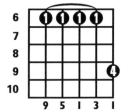
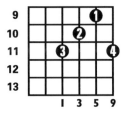

F#madd9
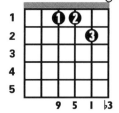
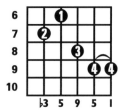
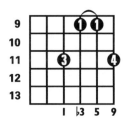

F#6add9
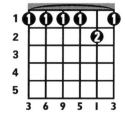
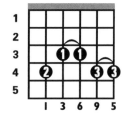
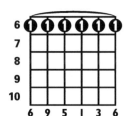

F#m6add9
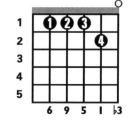
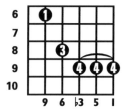
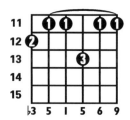

F#7-5
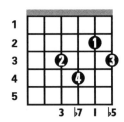
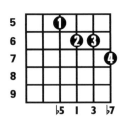
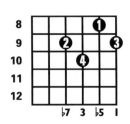

F#7+5
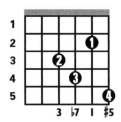
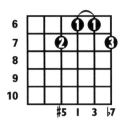
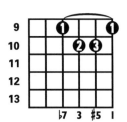

F#7-9
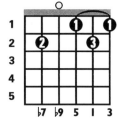
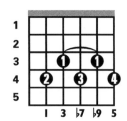
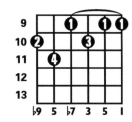

F#7+9
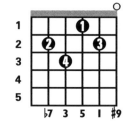
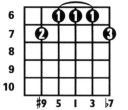
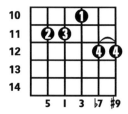

44

F#m(maj7)
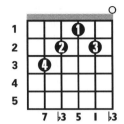
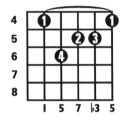
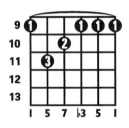

F#maj7-5
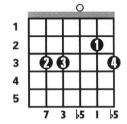
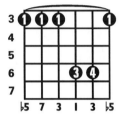
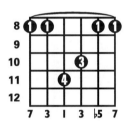

F#maj7+5

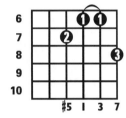
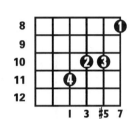

F#9
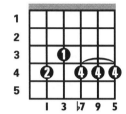
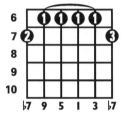
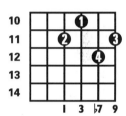

F#m9
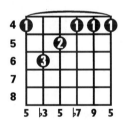
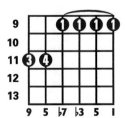
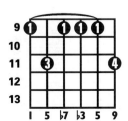

F#maj9

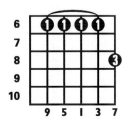

F#11
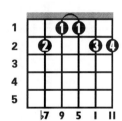
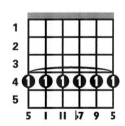
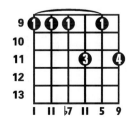

F#13
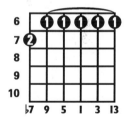
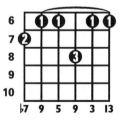
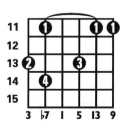

F#/ Gb Chords (Advanced)

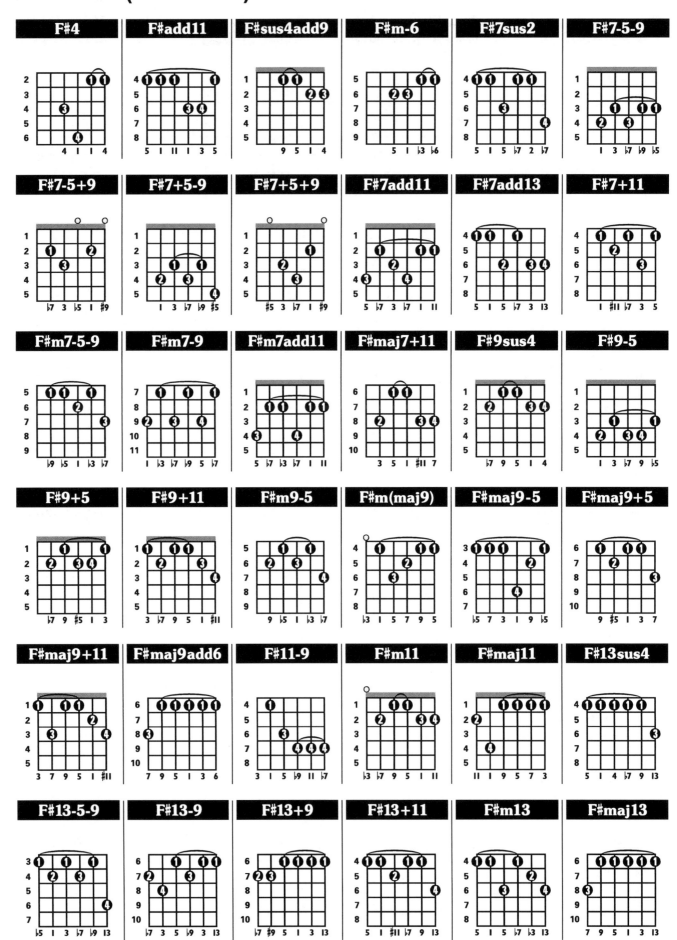

G

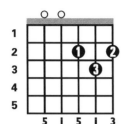
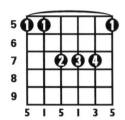
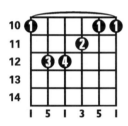

Gm

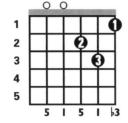
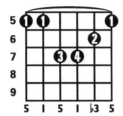
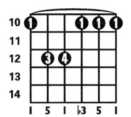

G7

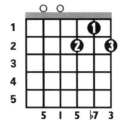
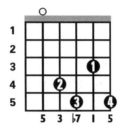
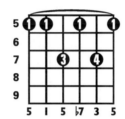

Gm7

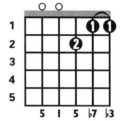
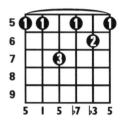
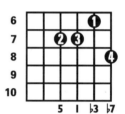

G5

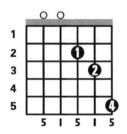
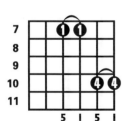
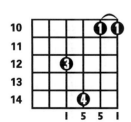

G6

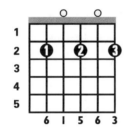
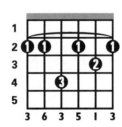
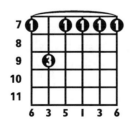

Gm6

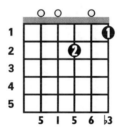
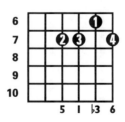
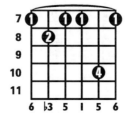

Gmaj7

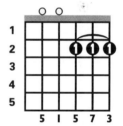
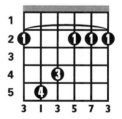
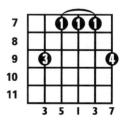

G Chords

Gº	Gº7	G-5	G+

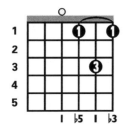
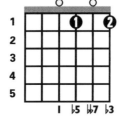
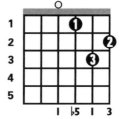
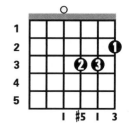

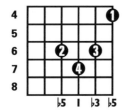
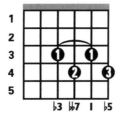
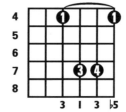
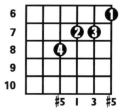

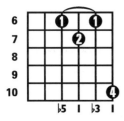
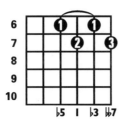
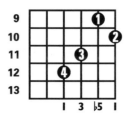
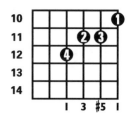

Gsus2	Gsus4	G7sus4	Gm7-5

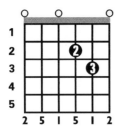
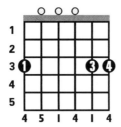
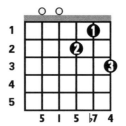
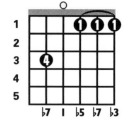

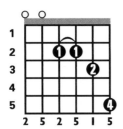
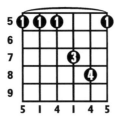
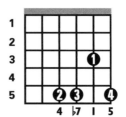
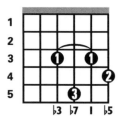

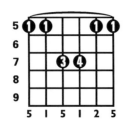
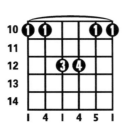
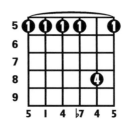
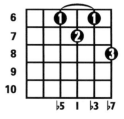

Gadd9

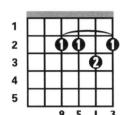

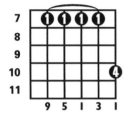

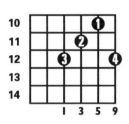

Gmadd9

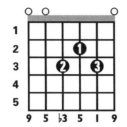

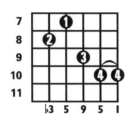

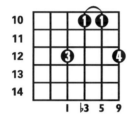

G6add9

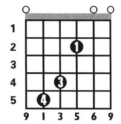

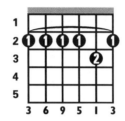

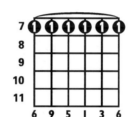

Gm6add9

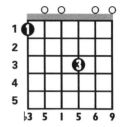

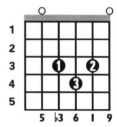

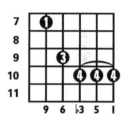

G7-5

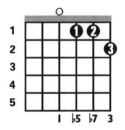

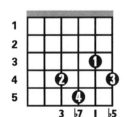

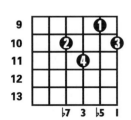

G7+5

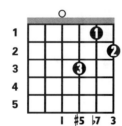

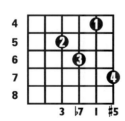

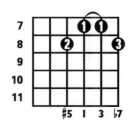

G7-9

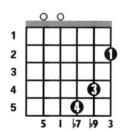

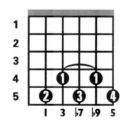

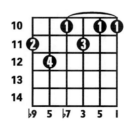

G7+9

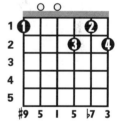

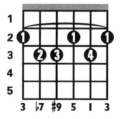

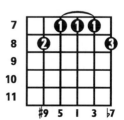

49

G Chords

Gm(maj7)

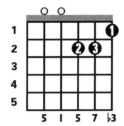

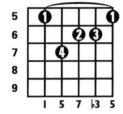

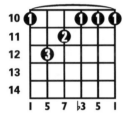

Gmaj7-5

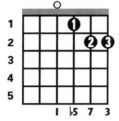

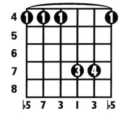

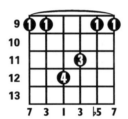

Gmaj7+5

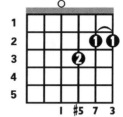

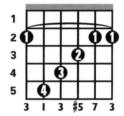

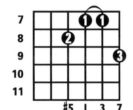

G9

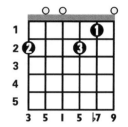

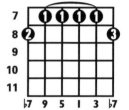

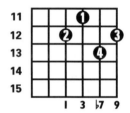

Gm9

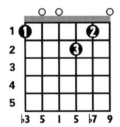

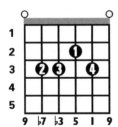

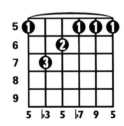

Gmaj9

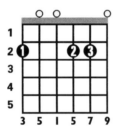

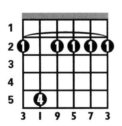

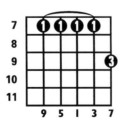

G11

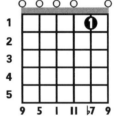

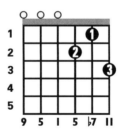

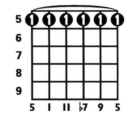

G13

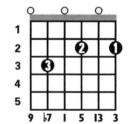

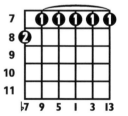

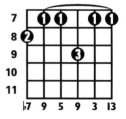

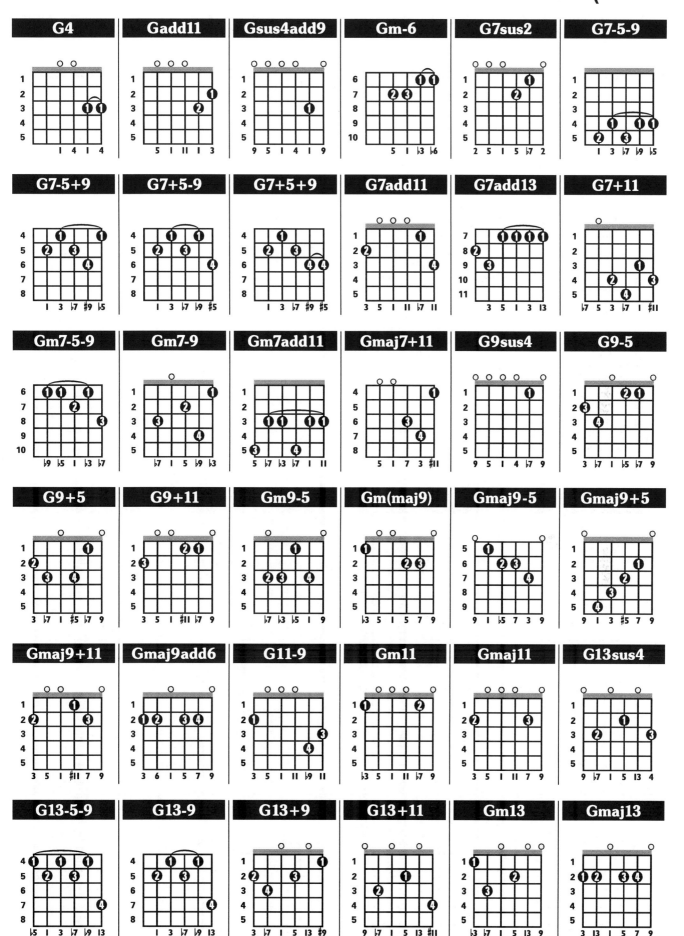

G# / A♭ Chords

A♭
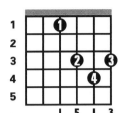
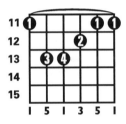
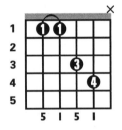

A♭m
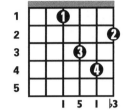
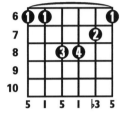
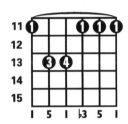

A♭7
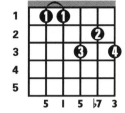
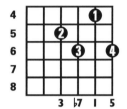
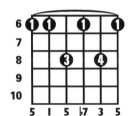

A♭m7
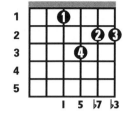
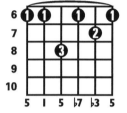
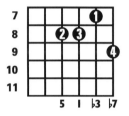

A♭5
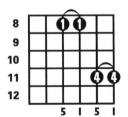
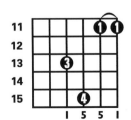

A♭6
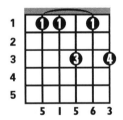
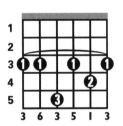
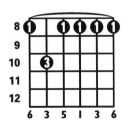

A♭m6
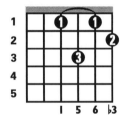
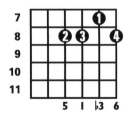
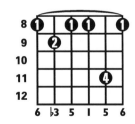

A♭maj7
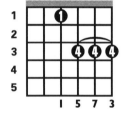
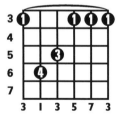
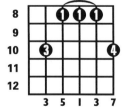

A♭°

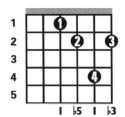

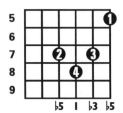

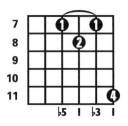

A♭°7

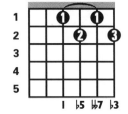

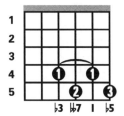

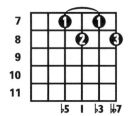

A♭-5

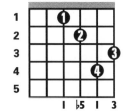

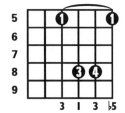

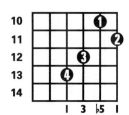

A♭+

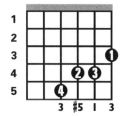

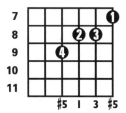

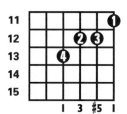

A♭sus2

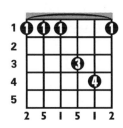

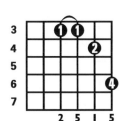

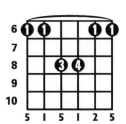

A♭sus4

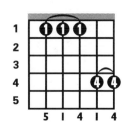

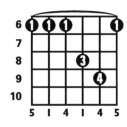

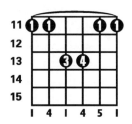

A♭7sus4

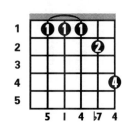

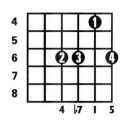

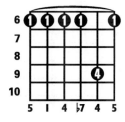

A♭m7-5

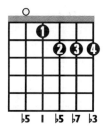

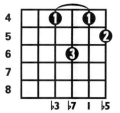

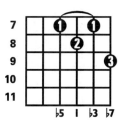

G# / A♭ Chords

A♭add9

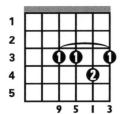

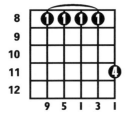

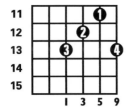

A♭madd9

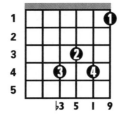

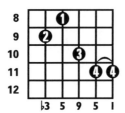

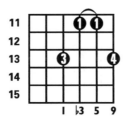

A♭6add9

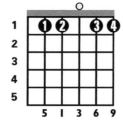

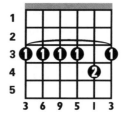

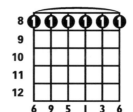

A♭m6add9

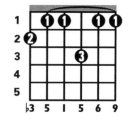

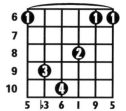

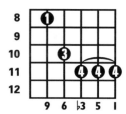

A♭7-5

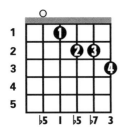

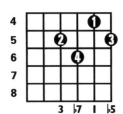

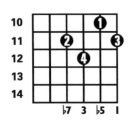

A♭7+5

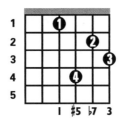

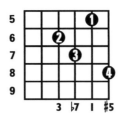

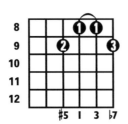

A♭7-9

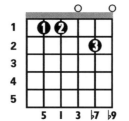

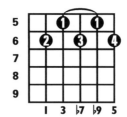

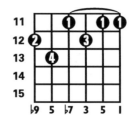

A♭7+9

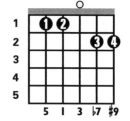

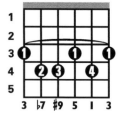

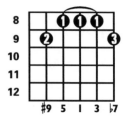

A♭m(maj7)

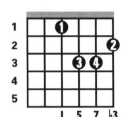

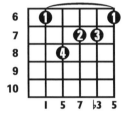

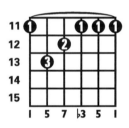

A♭maj7-5

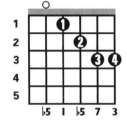

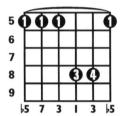

A♭maj7+5

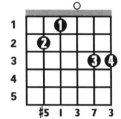

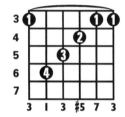

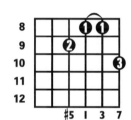

A♭9

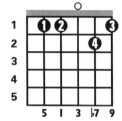

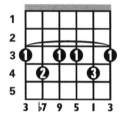

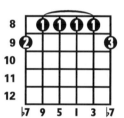

A♭m9

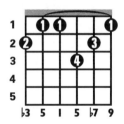

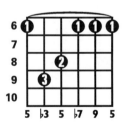

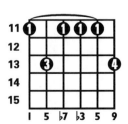

A♭maj9

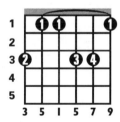

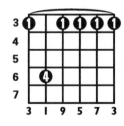

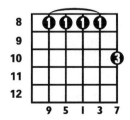

A♭11

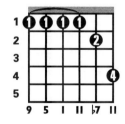

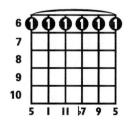

A♭13

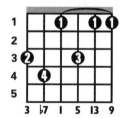

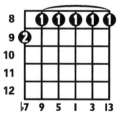

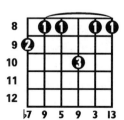

G# / A♭ Chords (Advanced)

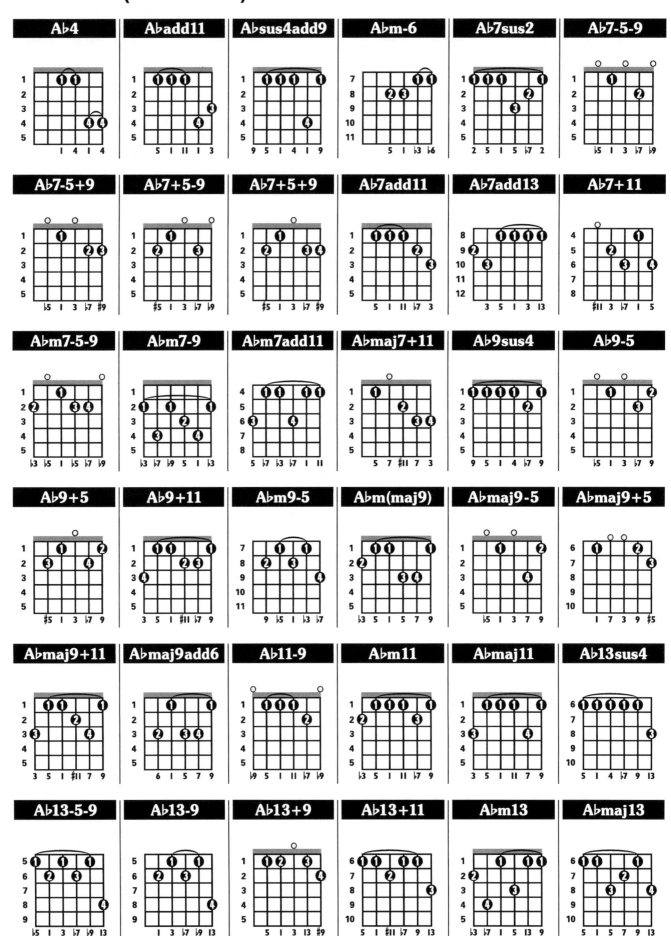

A	Am	A7	Am7
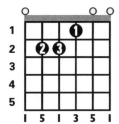	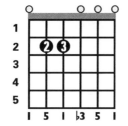	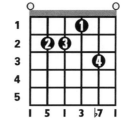	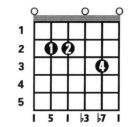
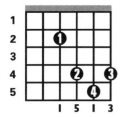	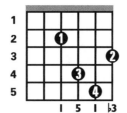	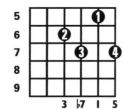	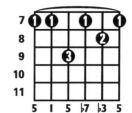
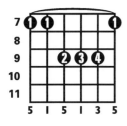	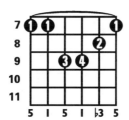	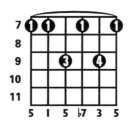	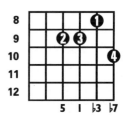

A5	A6	Am6	Amaj7
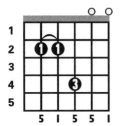	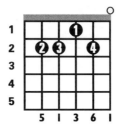	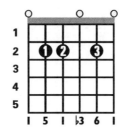	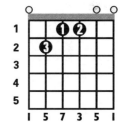
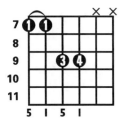	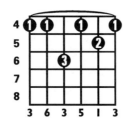	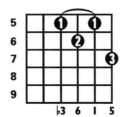	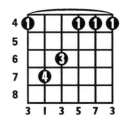
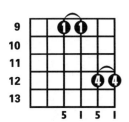	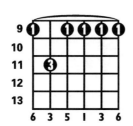	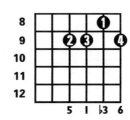	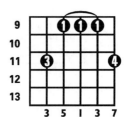

A Chords

A°	A°7	A-5	A+
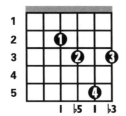	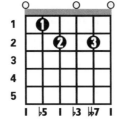	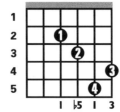	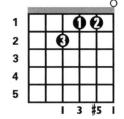
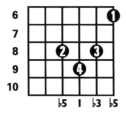	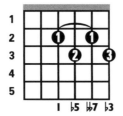	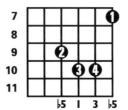	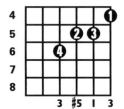
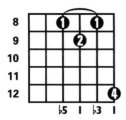	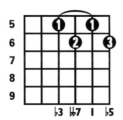	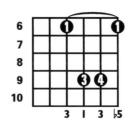	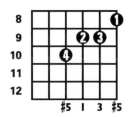

Asus2	Asus4	A7sus4	Am7-5
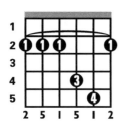	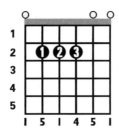	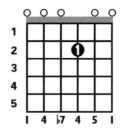	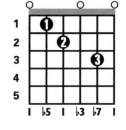
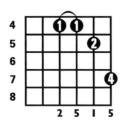	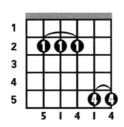	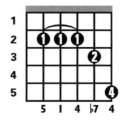	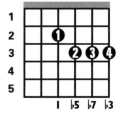
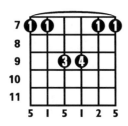	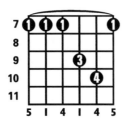	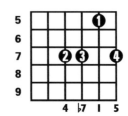	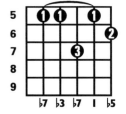

Aadd9

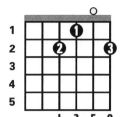

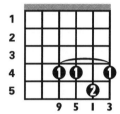

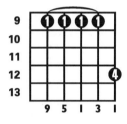

Amadd9

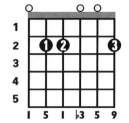

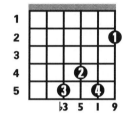

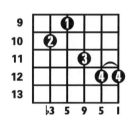

A6add9

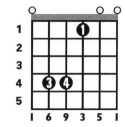

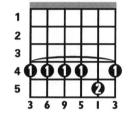

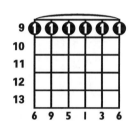

Am6add9

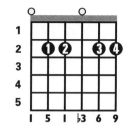

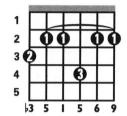

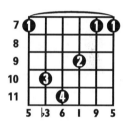

A7-5

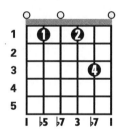

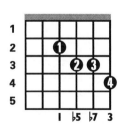

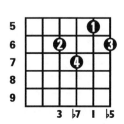

A7+5

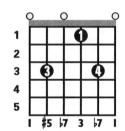

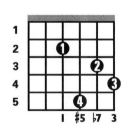

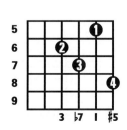

A7-9

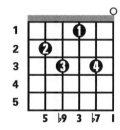

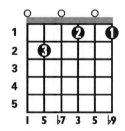

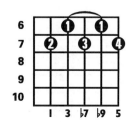

A7+9

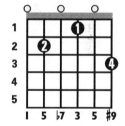

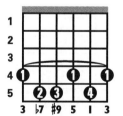

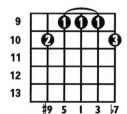

A Chords

Am(maj7)

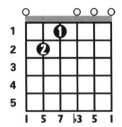

I 5 7 ♭3 5 I

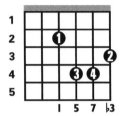

I 5 7 ♭3

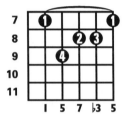

I 5 7 ♭3 5

Amaj7-5

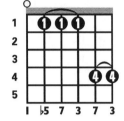

I ♭5 7 3 7 3

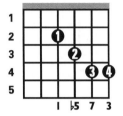

I ♭5 7 3

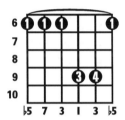

♭5 7 3 I 3 ♭5

Amaj7+5

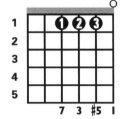

7 3 #5 I

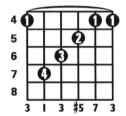

3 I 3 #5 7 3

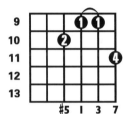

#5 I 3 7

A9

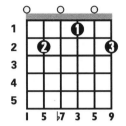

I 5 ♭7 3 5 9

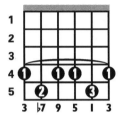

3 ♭7 9 5 I 3

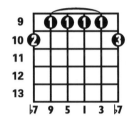

♭7 9 5 I 3 ♭7

Am9

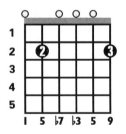

I 5 ♭7 ♭3 5 9

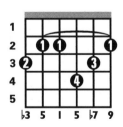

♭3 5 I 5 ♭7 9

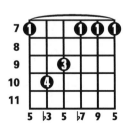

5 ♭3 5 ♭7 9 5

Amaj9

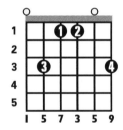

I 5 7 3 5 9

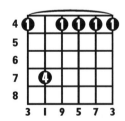

3 I 9 5 7 3

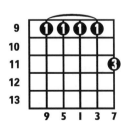

9 5 I 3 7

A11

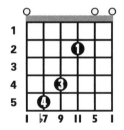

I ♭7 9 II 5 I

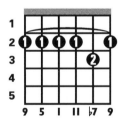

9 5 I II ♭7 9

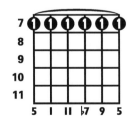

5 I II ♭7 9 5

A13

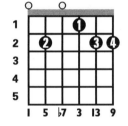

I 5 ♭7 3 13 9

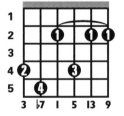

3 ♭7 I 5 13 9

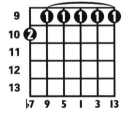

♭7 9 5 I 3 13

60

A Chords (Advanced)

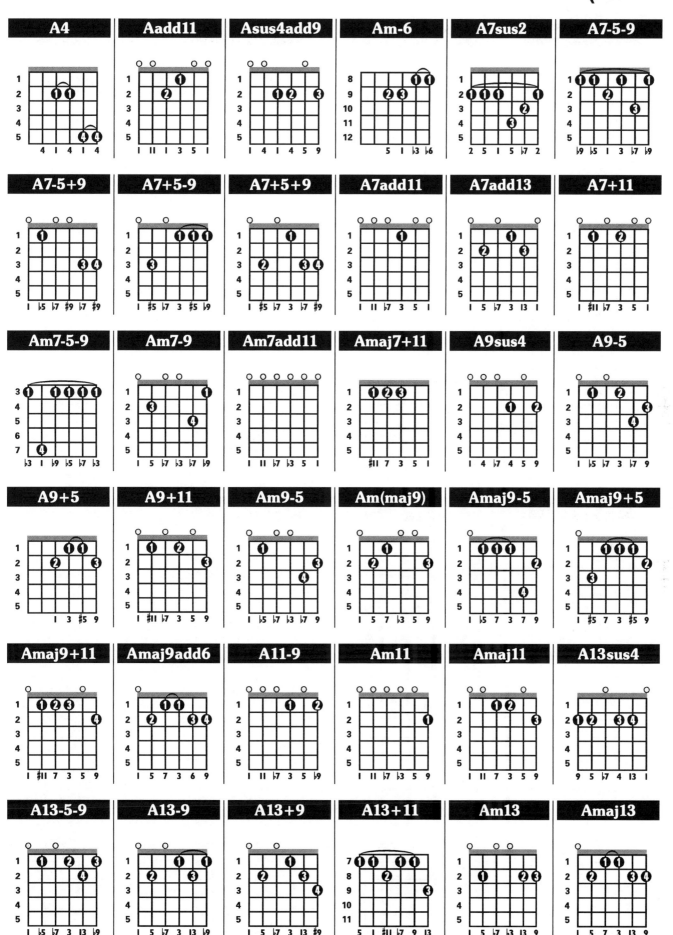

A# / B♭ Chords

B♭
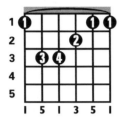
I 5 I 3 5 I

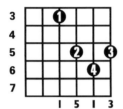
I 5 I 3

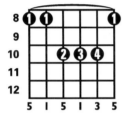
5 I 5 I 3 5

B♭m
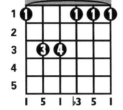
I 5 I ♭3 5 I

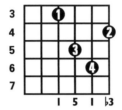
I 5 I ♭3

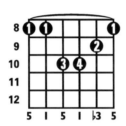
5 I 5 I ♭3 5

B♭7
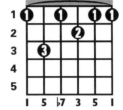
I 5 ♭7 3 5 I

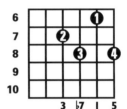
3 ♭7 I 5

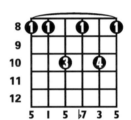
5 I 5 ♭7 3 5

B♭m7

I 5 ♭7 ♭3 5 I

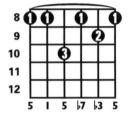
5 I 5 ♭7 ♭3 5

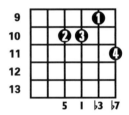
5 I ♭3 ♭7

B♭5
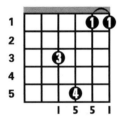
I 5 5 I

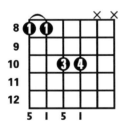
5 I 5 I

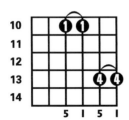
5 I 5 I

B♭6
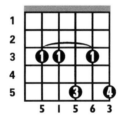
5 I 5 6 3

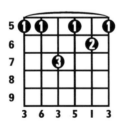
3 6 3 5 I 3

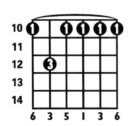
6 3 5 I 3 6

B♭m6
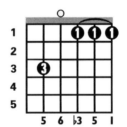
5 6 ♭3 5 I

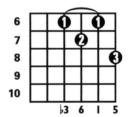
♭3 6 I 5

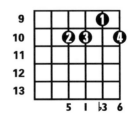
5 I ♭3 6

B♭maj7
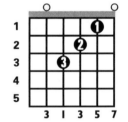
3 I 3 5 7

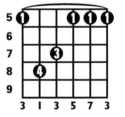
3 I 3 5 7 3

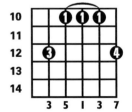
3 5 I 3 7

Bb°

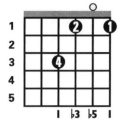

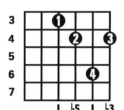

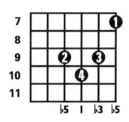

Bb°7

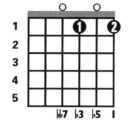

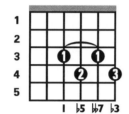

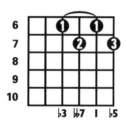

Bb-5

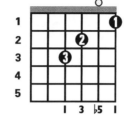

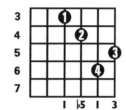

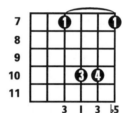

Bb+

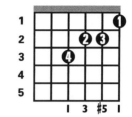

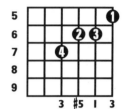

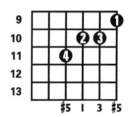

Bbsus2

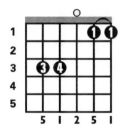

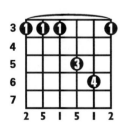

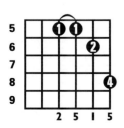

Bbsus4

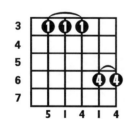

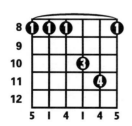

Bb7sus4

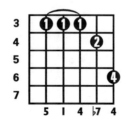

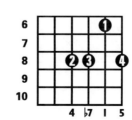

Bbm7-5

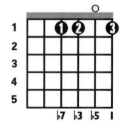

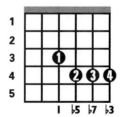

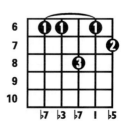

A# / B♭ Chords

B♭add9

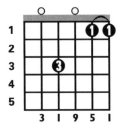

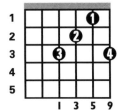

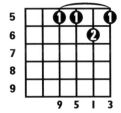

B♭madd9

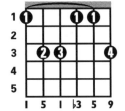

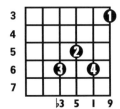

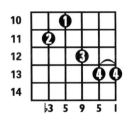

B♭6add9

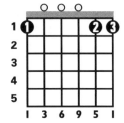

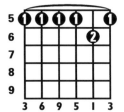

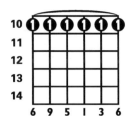

B♭m6add9

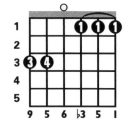

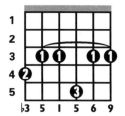

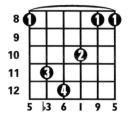

B♭7-5

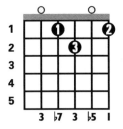

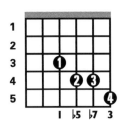

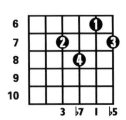

B♭7+5

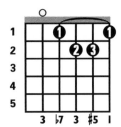

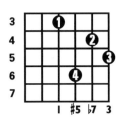

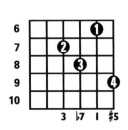

B♭7-9

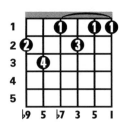

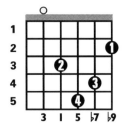

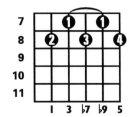

B♭7+9

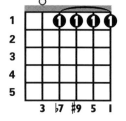

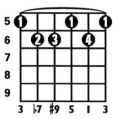

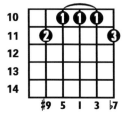

B♭m(maj7)

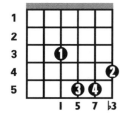

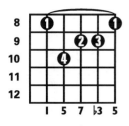

B♭maj7-5

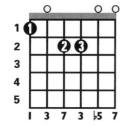

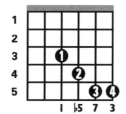

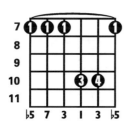

B♭maj7+5

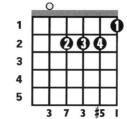

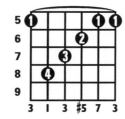

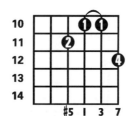

B♭9

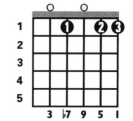

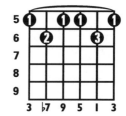

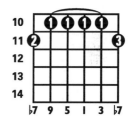

B♭m9

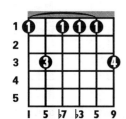

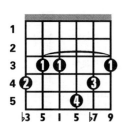

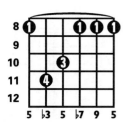

B♭maj9

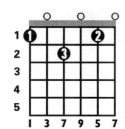

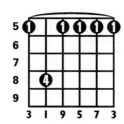

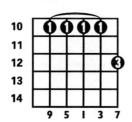

B♭11

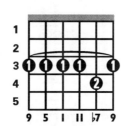

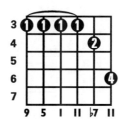

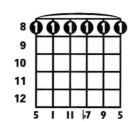

B♭13

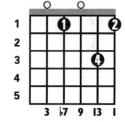

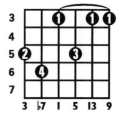

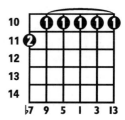

A# / B♭ Chords (Advanced)

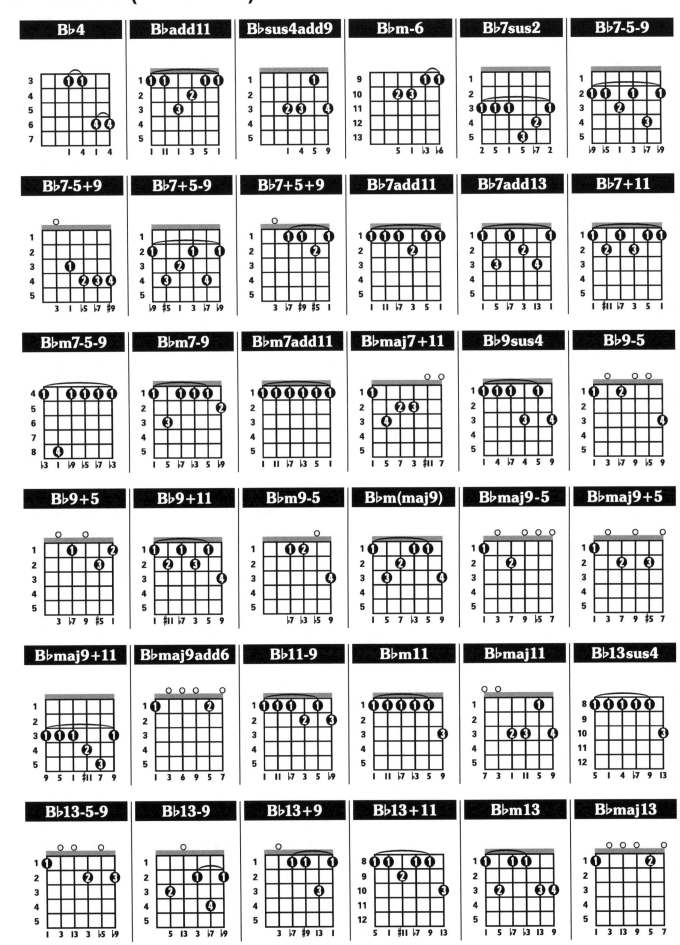

B Chords

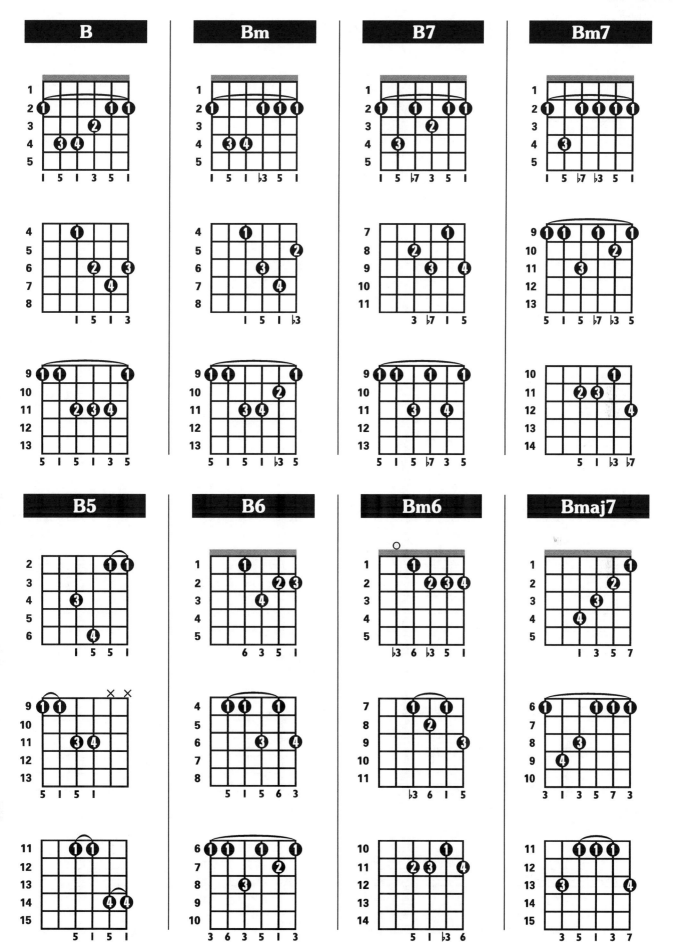

B Chords

Bº	Bº7	B-5	B+

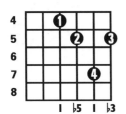
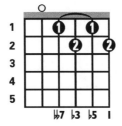
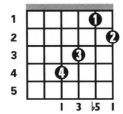
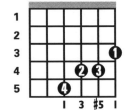

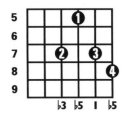
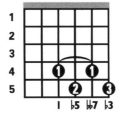
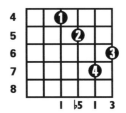
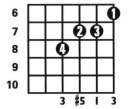

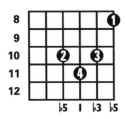
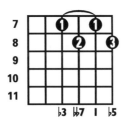
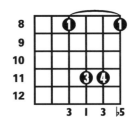
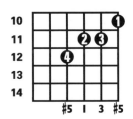

Bsus2	Bsus4	B7sus4	Bm7-5

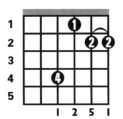
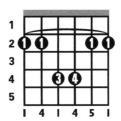
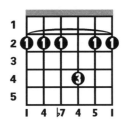
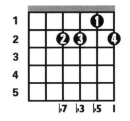

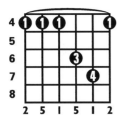
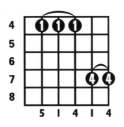
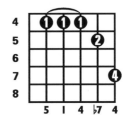
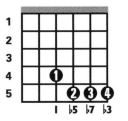

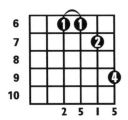
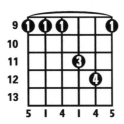
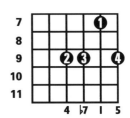
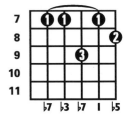

Badd9

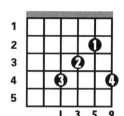

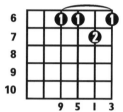

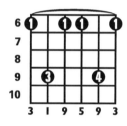

Bmadd9

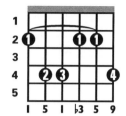

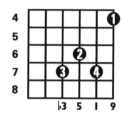

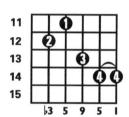

B6add9

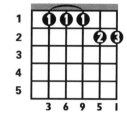

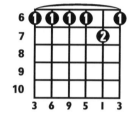

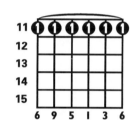

Bm6add9

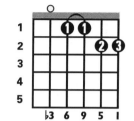

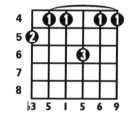

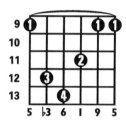

B7-5

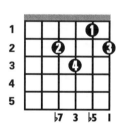

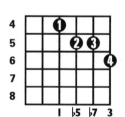

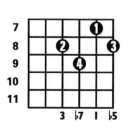

B7+5

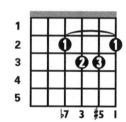

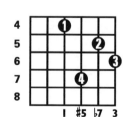

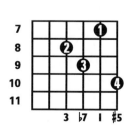

B7-9

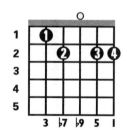

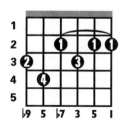

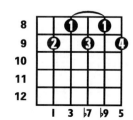

B7+9

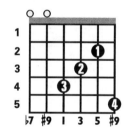

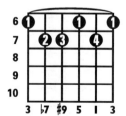

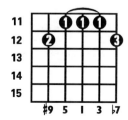

B Chords

Bm(maj7)
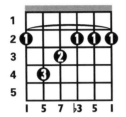
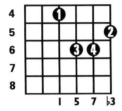
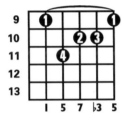

Bmaj7-5
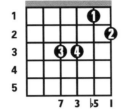
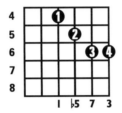
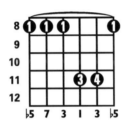

Bmaj7+5
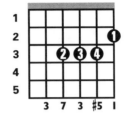
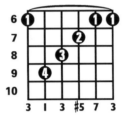
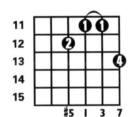

B9
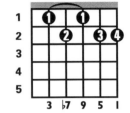
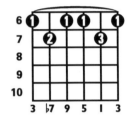
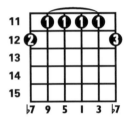

Bm9
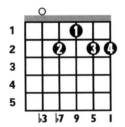
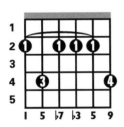
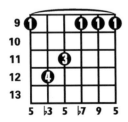

Bmaj9
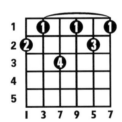
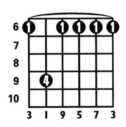
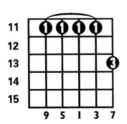

B11
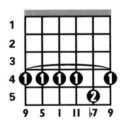
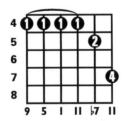
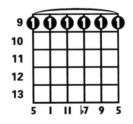

B13
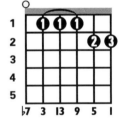
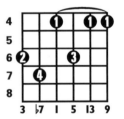
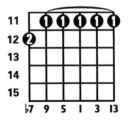

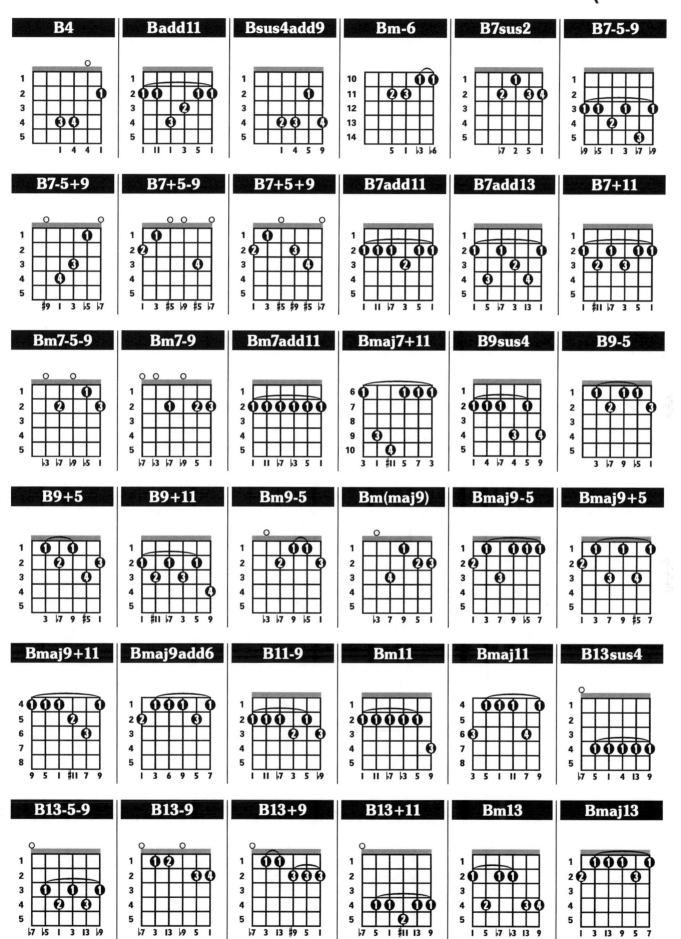

Major Slash Chords

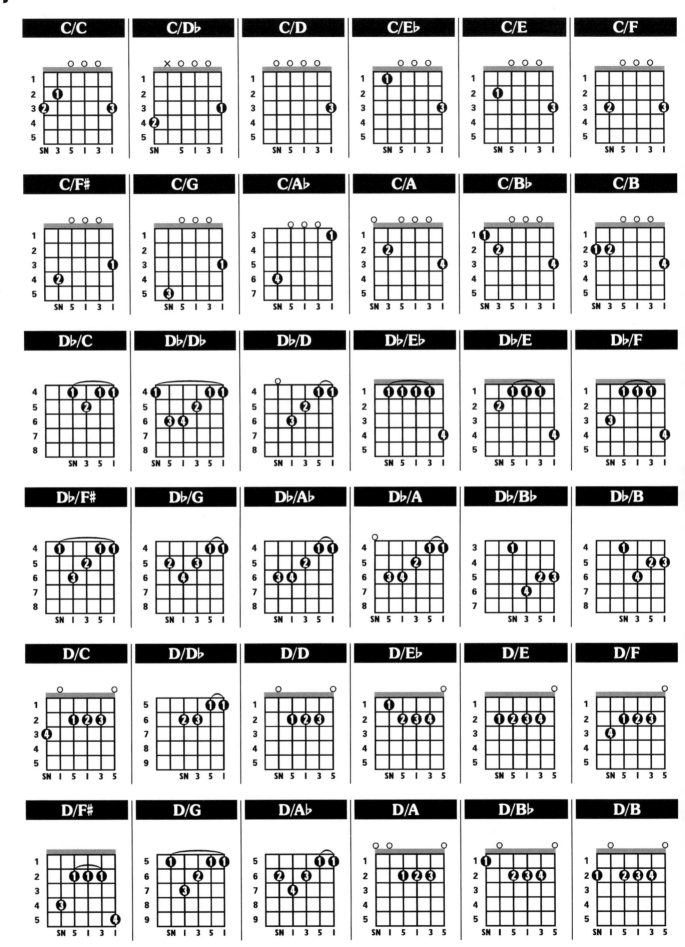

Major Slash Chords

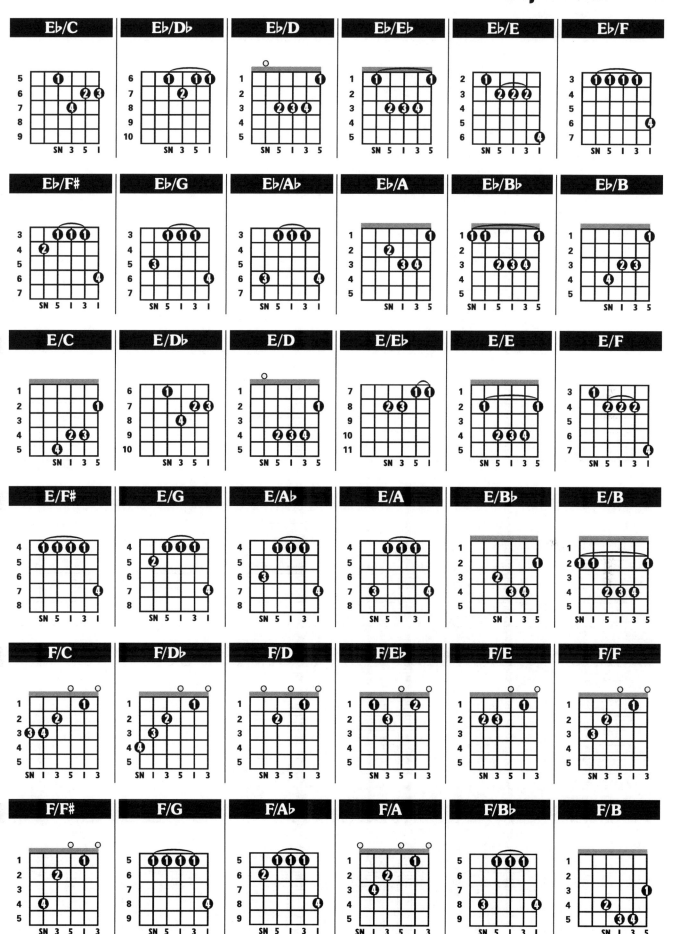

Major Slash Chords

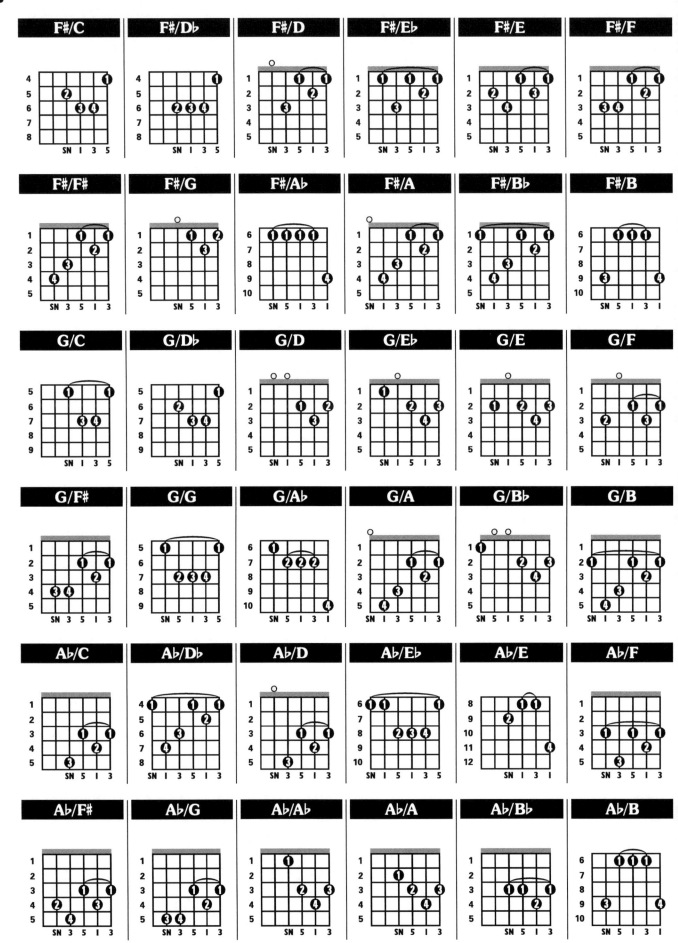

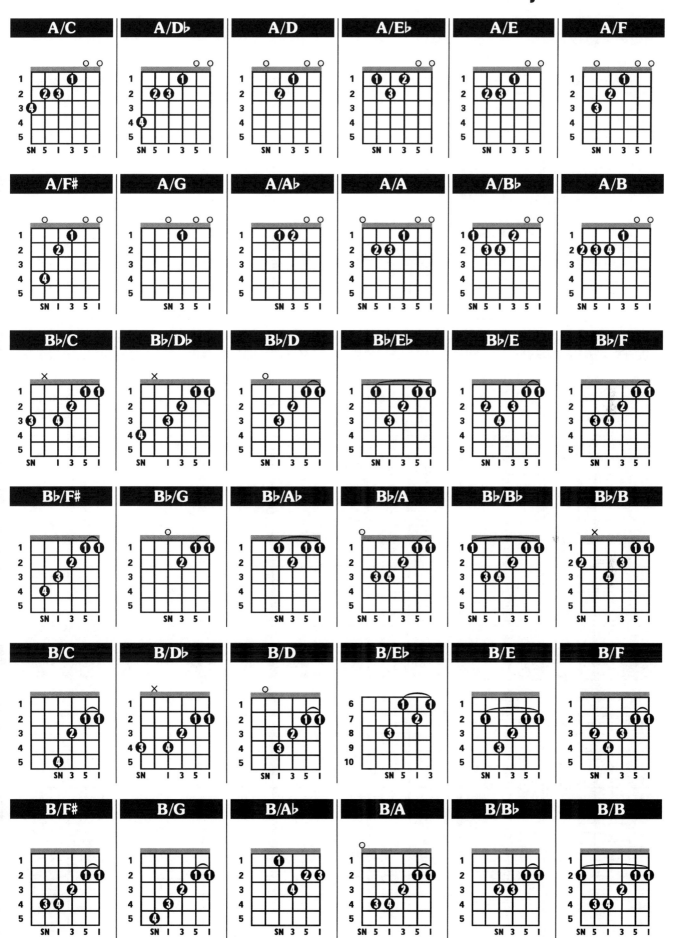

A Selection of Moveable Chord Shapes

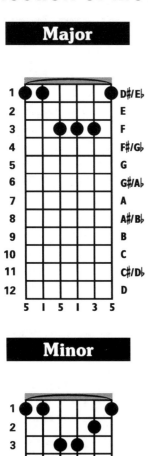
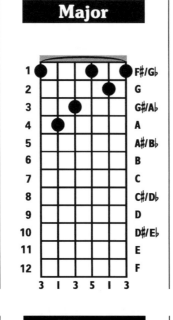
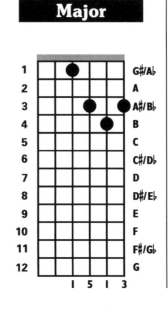
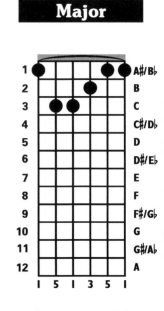

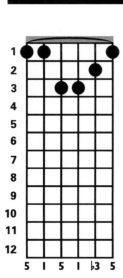
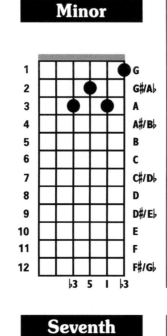
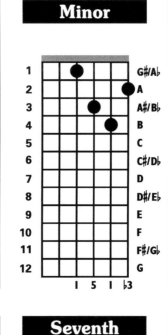
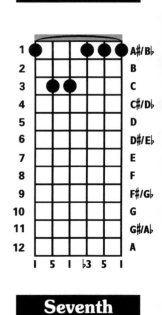

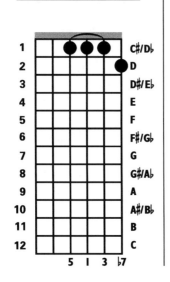
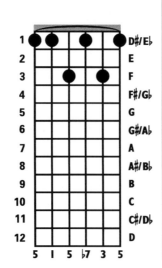
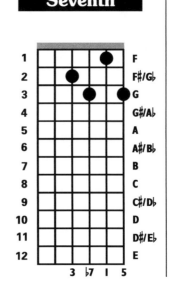
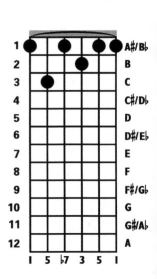

A Selection of Moveable Chord Shapes

Minor Seventh
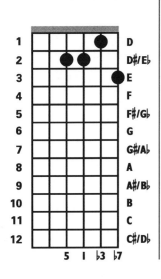

Minor Seventh
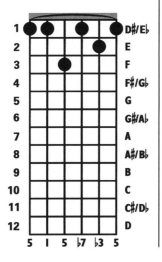

Minor Seventh
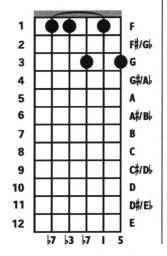

Minor Seventh
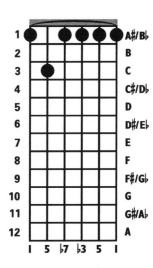

Sixth
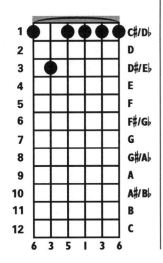

Sixth
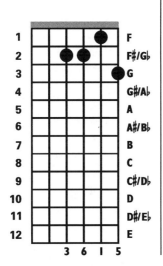

Sixth
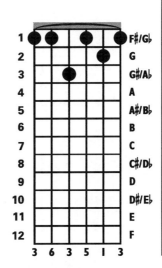

Sixth
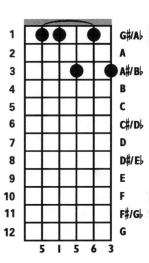

Minor Sixth
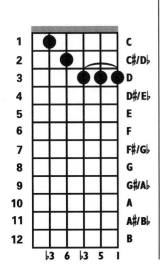

Minor Sixth
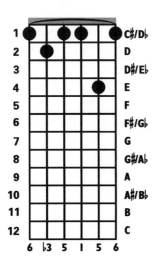

Minor Sixth
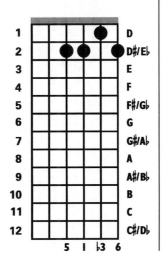

Minor Sixth
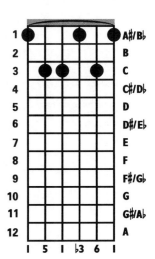

77

A Selection of Moveable Chord Shapes

Major Seventh
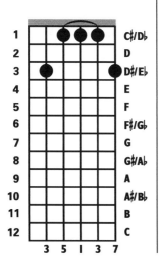

Major Seventh
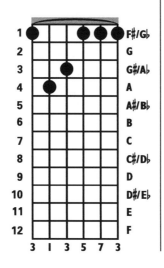

Major Seventh
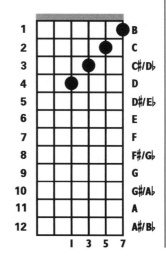

Suspended Fourth
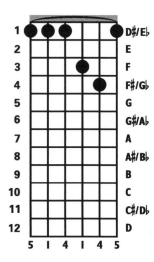

Suspended Fourth
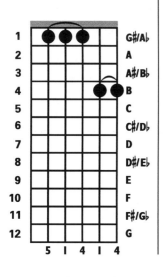

Suspended Fourth
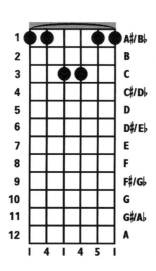

Diminished
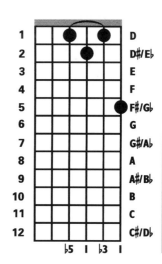

Diminished
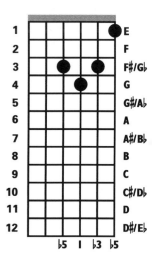

Diminished
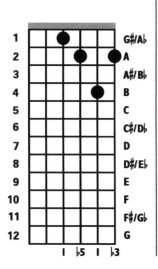

Augmented
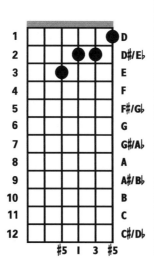

Augmented
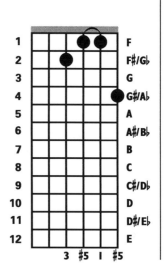

Augmented
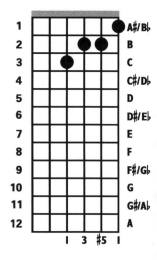

A Selection of Moveable Chord Shapes

Diminished Seventh

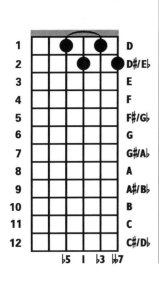

1	D
2	D#/Eb
3	E
4	F
5	F#/Gb
6	G
7	G#/Ab
8	A
9	A#/Bb
10	B
11	C
12	C#/Db

b5 I b3 bb7

Diminished Seventh

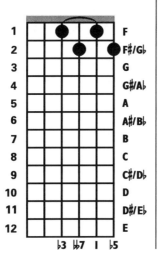

1	F
2	F#/Gb
3	G
4	G#/Ab
5	A
6	A#/Bb
7	B
8	C
9	C#/Db
10	D
11	D#/Eb
12	E

b3 bb7 I b5

Fifth

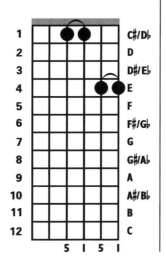

1	C#/Db
2	D
3	D#/Eb
4	E
5	F
6	F#/Gb
7	G
8	G#/Ab
9	A
10	A#/Bb
11	B
12	C

5 I 5 I

Fifth

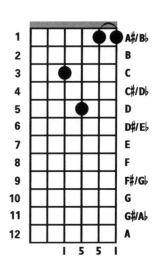

1	A#/Bb
2	B
3	C
4	C#/Db
5	D
6	D#/Eb
7	E
8	F
9	F#/Gb
10	G
11	G#/Ab
12	A

I 5 5 I

Seventh Suspended

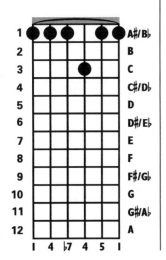

1	A#/Bb
2	B
3	C
4	C#/Db
5	D
6	D#/Eb
7	E
8	F
9	F#/Gb
10	G
11	G#/Ab
12	A

I 4 b7 4 5 I

Added Ninth

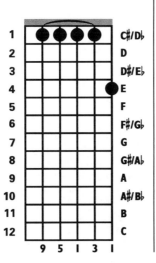

1	C#/Db
2	D
3	D#/Eb
4	E
5	F
6	F#/Gb
7	G
8	G#/Ab
9	A
10	A#/Bb
11	B
12	C

9 5 I 3 I

Added Ninth

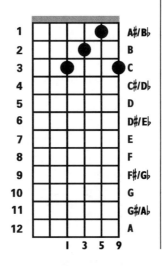

1	A#/Bb
2	B
3	C
4	C#/Db
5	D
6	D#/Eb
7	E
8	F
9	F#/Gb
10	G
11	G#/Ab
12	A

I 3 5 9

Ninth

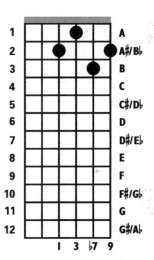

1	A
2	A#/Bb
3	B
4	C
5	C#/Db
6	D
7	D#/Eb
8	E
9	F
10	F#/Gb
11	G
12	G#/Ab

I 3 b7 9

Minor Ninth

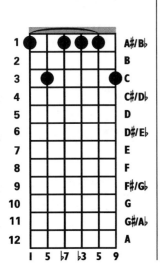

1	A#/Bb
2	B
3	C
4	C#/Db
5	D
6	D#/Eb
7	E
8	F
9	F#/Gb
10	G
11	G#/Ab
12	A

I 5 b7 b3 5 9

Major Ninth

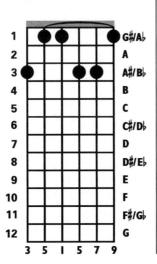

1	G#/Ab
2	A
3	A#/Bb
4	B
5	C
6	C#/Db
7	D
8	D#/Eb
9	E
10	F
11	F#/Gb
12	G

3 5 I 5 7 9

Eleventh

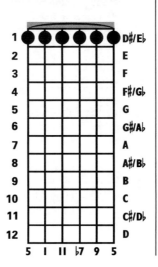

1	D#/Eb
2	E
3	F
4	F#/Gb
5	G
6	G#/Ab
7	A
8	A#/Bb
9	B
10	C
11	C#/Db
12	D

5 I 11 b7 9 5

Thirteenth

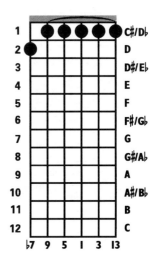

1	C#/Db
2	D
3	D#/Eb
4	E
5	F
6	F#/Gb
7	G
8	G#/Ab
9	A
10	A#/Bb
11	B
12	C

b7 9 5 I 3 13

THE GUITAR & UKULELE FAMILY FACTFILE

Acoustic Guitar, Folk Guitar or Flat-Top Guitar

Where the acoustic flat-top guitar differs from its earlier classical cousin is in the use of steel strings. Its evolution, although roughly based on earlier European classical designs, can be found in early twentieth century America. Perhaps unsurprisingly, the names of *Martin* and *Gibson* were hugely influential in the designs we see today. Although changes have taken place over the years, the fundamental shape and construction methods have remained very similar. Types of acoustic include:

Dreadnought: The popular large bodied *Dreadnought* acoustics were first produced by *Martin* in 1931, based on designs dating back to an earlier series by the *Ditson* company of Boston. *Martin* discarded the internal fan bracing found on the *Ditson* models and replaced it with the ground breaking X-bracing found on the majority of their instruments today. The name Dreadnought was coined by *Martin* in 1931 after the British battleship, *H.M.S. Dreadnaught*.

Jumbo: A typical jumbo guitar such as the famous *Gibson J-200* has a much more pinched-in waist than the dreadnought, with rounder shoulders and rounder lower bout. This leviathan of the guitar world as you might expect from it's large body, has the greatest bass response of any acoustic guitar.

Concert, *Grand Concert* and *Auditorium Size*: These acoustics feature a much smaller overall body area compared with the Jumbo and Dreadnought, but can be surprisingly loud for their size.

Travel & Backpacker: Guitars with a highly compressed body sized suitable for the travelling musician.

Important manufacters of the acoustic guitar include: *C.F. Martin, Gibson, Guild, Ovation, Taylor, Takamine, Fylde, Maccaferri, Yamaha, Alvarez, Seagull* among others.

Akulele

A new design of ukulele carved from a single piece of wood, much like the construction of the Andean charango. The Akulele comes in a variety of configurations including a taropatch model and a higher pitched sopranino, which has a shorter scale than the soprano and is tuned a fifth higher (D-G-B-E). With it's origins coming out of the marriage between ukulele and charango, the sopranino could be compared to the relationship between the charango and its little sibling, the walaycho.

Archtop Guitar

The design of the archtop owes most of its basic characteristics to European violin luthery. Much like the violin family, the archtop has a curved soundboard and f-holes for sound projection. Over the years the archtop's remained a popular choice among jazz guitarists in both it's acoustic and semi-acoustic incarnations. Popular manufacturers of the archtop over the years have included: *Gibson, Epiphone, Martin, D'Angelico and Vega*.

Bajo Sexto & Bajo Quinto

The bajo sexto is an instrument of Mexican origin providing the bass rhythm accompaniment for the accordian in a typical *Conjunto/Norteño* or *Tejano* band. It features 12 strings in 6 courses, a little like a lower pitched 12-string guitar. The first three courses of strings are paired in unison, with the last three strung in octaves in E-A-D-G-C-F tuning (low to high). Its sister instrument, the quinto appeared in recent years as an alternative to the sexto because bajo players often remove the lowest course of strings anyway, as they feel it tends to muddy the sound. The origin of the instrument is not altogether clear, but it's thought the bajo was first created in Spain and brought to Mexico in the latter part of the 19th century to the Bajio region of Jalisco.

Baritone Guitar

The baritone was originally created by the *Danelectro* company in the 1950s but intially struggled to find favour with musicians. Gradually, though, it found a niche in musical genres as diverse as surf music, country and movie tracks where its lower range was successfully added to the sound for dramatic musical effect. The scale length of a typical baritone is a little longer than a standard guitar to allow for the lower tuning. Most baritones are generally tuned to a 5th (A-D-G-C-E-A) or a 4th (B-E-A-D-F#-B) lower than standard tuning, but some players prefer to go as far as an octave lower (E-A-D-G-B-E). Manufacturers and independent luthiers include: *Fender, Gretsch, Danelectro, Ellis, Goodall, Santa Cruz, Manzer, Galloup, Berkowitz, Mustapick and Veillette*.

Baritone Ukulele

The big brother of the ukulele family first appeared in 1940s America, many decades after it's soprano forebear. The idea behind the baritone uke was said to have been thought up by U.S. variety show host and ukulele player, Arthur Godfrey, a major star at the birth of popular television. Although it could be argued, the baritone is more like a four stringed guitar than a traditional uke, its remained a popular minority instrument ever since it's inception. The baritone uke is tuned to an open G6 chord (D-G-B-E), a fourth lower than standard ukulele C6 tuning.

Baroque Guitar

The classical guitar owes much of it's evolution to its smaller 5-course baroque ancestor. A typical baroque guitar was strung in double courses and only switched to the single coursed instrument we know today during the early Romantic era. The instrument was strung with gut strings while the frets were tied to the neck, very much like the European lute. The most famous image of a baroque guitar being played can be seen in Jan Vermeer's painting, *The Guitar Player* (c.1672). The tuning was identical to today's standard guitar configuration, minus the 6th E string, with a few variations for octave pairs (A-D-G-B-E).

Bass Guitar

The first electric horizontal fretted bass was designed by Seattle inventor Paul Tutmarc in the 1930s. But it wasn't until Leo Fender created the first mass production model in 1951, the famous *Precision Bass*, that the instrument really found a home in popular music. Although the upright bass still finds significant favour within today's various musical genres, the electric has for many years been the choice of most musicians. In recent years, the acoustic horizontal bass (first designed in the 1970s by *Ernie Ball*) and electric 5,6,7,8,10 and 12-string variations have been added to the bassists armoury. Important models include: *The Fender Precision* and *Jazz Basses*, the *Gibson EB Series*, the *Rickenbacker 4001*, *Hofner Violin bass*, *Steinberger headless L-Series* and the beautifully crafted, but expensive *Alembic* range.

Battente Guitar or Chitarra Battente

An Italian steel strung design of guitar popular during the mid 1500s. The battente generally had fixed frets and either a fixed or floating bridge with tailpiece arrangement.

Braguinha

A Madeiran instrument said to have been the main ancestor of today's ukulele. The Braguinha features the same scale length as a standard soprano uke, but is tuned roughly a fourth lower to an open G major chord (D-G-B-D). The name of the instrument itself is taken from the Madeiran city of Braga.

Cavaquinho

The cavaquinho is probably best known for its role in Brazilian samba and choro music, where it's played with a pick, using a rhythmical strumming technique. Standard tuning is generally considered to be based on a G major open chord (D-G-B-D). Other popular tunings include G-G-B-D (again, another inversion of the open G major) and A-A-C#-E (open A major chord). D-G-B-E is also used, particularly by guitarists. This tuning is shared with the baritone uke. Apart from Brazil, this little uke-sized instrument can be found in Madeira, The Azores, Cape Verde, Hawaii and other locations where Portuguese immigration has had a sizeable impact.

Charango

Although the charango isn't strictly a member of the ukulele family, it shares many attributes with its Hawaiian cousin, including re-entrant tuning, plus an additional high course (G-C-E-A-E). Again, like the soprano uke, it's tuned to an open C6 chord, but features double nylon courses of strings instead of singles. The original charangos were made from the shells of the poor unfortunate armadillo or *quirquincho*. Fortunately, today this practice is dying out, with most instrument bodies being constructed from indigenous woods from the Andean region of South America. The body shape of the charango also differs from the uke, featuring a rounded back, reflecting its armadillo shell ancestry.

The charango, much like the ukulele is also part of a larger family group. The charango is pitched in the soprano range, while the ronroco (or *ronrroco*) is a full octave lower, the charangon a fourth or a fifth lower and the walaycho (*hualaycho*, *waylacho* or *maulincho*), a fourth or a fifth higher. All generally feature nylon strings, except the walaycho which sometimes utilizes steel strings.

Cigarbox Guitar

As the name suggests, a guitar or guitar-like instrument built from a cigarbox for the body or other non-traditional materials. These home-made folk-style instruments have a not inconsiderable following among enthusiasts of the style. An allied form is the cookie tin banjo, again built from non-traditional household materials.

Classical Guitar

The history of the classical guitar can be traced back to its baroque counterpart, with further influences from the gittern (*or renaissance guitar*), vihuela and European lute. But the 6-string version we know today can be more accurately attributed to Gaetano Vinaccia, a Neopolitan luthier who built the first recognisable model in 1779. Vinaccia came from a family of luthiers who had a big hand in the development of the mandolin.

Originally the classical guitar was strung with gut strings, but since the development of plastics, most musicians use nylon, carbon fibre or other composite materials. Physically, the classical's most obvious difference from other styles of guitar is in the use of a wider fretboard. This is necessary to accomodate the fingerstyle of playing associated with the classical repetoire. The instrument we know today has remained more or less the same for the last hundred years in terms of size and shape. Construction of the top models generally features a Western red cedar or spruce top, rosewood back and sides and a Spanish cedar or mahogany neck, with ebony fingerboard. Major manufacturers and makers include: *Ramirez, Barbero, Fernandez, Hirade, Asturias, Takamine, Almansa* and *Contreras*.

Concert Ukulele

The first concert ukulele appeared in 1925 as a result of the Martin guitar company failing to sell sufficient quantities of its 8-string taropatch model. The solution was a simple one. The double courses were removed and the larger bodied concert uke was born. Today the concert model slots in between the soprano and tenor models in terms of size. The tuning is identical to the soprano.

Dobro, Resonator *or* Resophonic Guitar

The *Dobro* or resonator guitar was first developed in the 1920s by five Czechoslovakian immigrant brothers, the Dopyeras (the name was later Americanized to Dopera). The first resonator model was a tricone *National* guitar probably designed by John Dopyera. Together with George Beauchamp, Adolph Rickenbacker and others, he formed The *National Guitar Company* in 1925. The resonating chamber of this innovative

instrument consisted of 3 metal cones set in a triangular configuration, joined to a 3-legged bridge arrangement. These were then set into the all-metal body of the guitar. The instrument remains popular to this day, mainly with blues players.

The actual single cone *Dobro* design appeared a little later around 1928-29, again by John Dopyera who had to design a new resonator to avoid patent clashes with *National's* tricone models. The new design consisted of an inverted single resonating cone, where the strings rested on a cast aluminium *spider* (so-called because of its 8 legs!), which in turn sat around the outside rim of the cone. The complete history of this instrument is long and complicated and would probably be a book in itself! The true wooden-bodied single cone *Dobro* is the instrument of choice for most bluegrass players.

Major manufacturers of the resonator guitar include: *National, Dobro (now Gibson-owned), Regal, Epiphone* and others.

Drumtar

A bizarre mixture of guitar and snare drum, where the head vibrates when a string is strummed or picked. Visually, they look a bit like a banjo.

Electric Solid-Body and Semi-Acoustic Guitar

Historically, the electric guitar came about through the need for greater volume within a big band setting. Being unable to compete with the dynamics of a full blown brass section, the electromagnetic transducer was invented and fitted to archtop guitars, which in turn ran through an early amplification system. Over the next few years, development continued with companies like *Rickenbacker* who produced the forerunner of the solid bodied electric, the aptly named *Frying Pan* lap lap steel. The 1940s saw musician and inventor Les Paul design his first guitar, which became unflatteringly known as the *Log*. But within a few short years he would go on and design the guitar that bears his name and is still undoubtedly one of the most popular designs ever created - The *Les Paul*. The following decade saw the first commercially viable solid bodied electric in the form of the *Fender Esquire*, a single magnetic pickup model later to be released in twin pickup form as the *Broadcaster*. This in turn was re-named the *Fender Telecaster* and the rest, as they, is history. But in 1954 Leo Fender came up with his greatest ever design. The *Stratocaster* was originally produced as a deluxe model and was pitched as one step up from the slightly more modest *Telecaster*. Its popularity unsurprisingly grew and went on to become a full production model with its innovative use of the vibrato arm, triple pickup system and double cutaways. Today, electric guitar design still owes much of its allegiance to the likes of Paul and Fender, but new ideas such as software guitar modelling, sampling and synthesis have found their way into the guitarists locker - a domain formally occupied with some exclusivity by the keyboard player. Leading designs over the years have included: The *Fender Telecaster* and *Stratocaster*, the *Gibson Les Paul, SG, Explorer, Firebird* and *Flying V*.

English Guittar *or* English Guitar

The term English guitar is actually something of a misnomer. This 6-course, 10-stringed instrument should more accurately be classed as a form of cittern. It's popularity ran from the 1750s up until the 19th century where it was used as a parlour-style instrument. The only instruments you're likely to see today are luthier built reproduction models, although a few originals do still appear from time to time. The tuning of the English guittar is set to an C major chord (C-E-G-C-E-G).

Flamenco Guitar

In many ways, the flamenco guitar resembles a standard classical model, but with a few important differences. Firstly, the flamenco is a little smaller and lighter in comparison with a brighter tonality to the sound. This is important for the guitar to cut through and contrast against the characteristic clicking of the dancer's nailed shoes. To protect the top against damage, a tap plate or *golpeador* is generally added. This is similar to a pick guard or scratch plate and helps to emphasize the *golpes* or finger taps. The main visible difference, though, is in the headstock, where most models of flamenco guitar feature a traditional peghead configuration, rather than geared tuners favoured by classical guitarists. This is to improve the sustaining qualities of the instrument by adding more weight to the head. The action on a flamenco is also quite a bit lower to make the playing of rapid *picado* passages a lot easier. It also helps to produce the familiar fret buzz which is an important constituent part of flamenco playing. The construction of most flamencos is either from Spanish cyprus or spruce. Leading flamenco guitarists include: Paco Peña, Juan Martin, Paco de Lucia, Ramón Montoya, Tomatito, Vicente Amigo Girol, Sabicas, Oscar Herrero, Rafael and Manolo Sanlucar.

Guitar Banjo
Unfairly, the guitar banjo is looked on as something of a novelty instrument for guitarists who have little wish to put the hours in to learn to play the real thing. This is unfortunate as this banjo variant is very much an instrument in its own right, with all the versatility of the six courses thrown in. Most players tend to use standard guitar tuning, but other configurations such as DADGAD or Drop D are just as valid. Predictably, as night follows day, 12-string versions of the guitar banjo have also appeared over the years. The sound is probably best described as *jingle-jangle-plunk!* The most famous exponent on the guitar banjo was probably the great jazz banjoist, *Johnny St. Cyr.* Other notable players include: *Danny Barker, Papa Charlie Jackson* and *Clancy Hayes.*

Guitalele, Guitarlele, Guilele or Kīkū
A popular modern hybrid instrument, incorporating the portability and size of a tenor or baritone ukulele with the transposed tuning of a 6-string guitar. The guitalele is tuned ADGCEA, like a standard soprano uke with two added 5th and 6th strings or a guitar capoed at the fifth fret. It shares a tuning with it's bigger cousin, the requinto, which is a much physically larger instrument, with a deep resonant body.

The guitalele makes an ideal introductory instrument for children or as travel guitar, because of it's conveniently transportable small size and playability for smaller fingers. Luthery companies that make their own versions of the guitalele include: *Yamaha, Gretsch, Mele, Koaloha, Cordoba, Kanile, Lichty, Kinnard and Islander.*

Guitarrón
A large bodied fretless bass instrument found in Mexican *Mariachi* music. The guitarrón usually has a scale length of between 650mm and 750mm, strung over a deep resonating body chamber. The tuning of this string bass proportioned instrument is A-D-G-C-E-A.

Harp Guitar
The history of the harp guitar goes back at least two centuries. To qualify for this description, the instrument generally has to feature a regular fretted guitar with a set of additional unstopped or unfretted lower pitched strings attached to a harp-like column nearest to the player's chin. American designs tend to include hollow columns or arms in a harp style and sometimes double necks.

Lap Steel Guitar, Table Steel Guitar & Pedal Steel Guitar
What differentiates this form of guitar from other instruments in the family is the flat or lap-style position of the player. The lap steel guitar tends to rest on the player's thighs, while its siblings, the table and pedal steel are raised up to sitting position on four tubular metal legs. The other common link between these guitars is the raised nut/bridge configuration. This is to stop the strings coming in contact with the fretboard when a *slide* or *steel* is used. A lap steel guitar generally features

6 strings, whereas a table steel often has 8 in a twin, triple or quad-ruple-neck configuration. The pedal steel is available in either single or twin-neck designs and utilizes a series of pedals and knee levers to change the tuning during a performance. Each neck can have anything between 8 and 14 strings. Unlike some lap steels the pedal variety is purely electric and has to rely on external amplification. The pedal steel guitar is particularly popular in country music, while the lap steel has always been a mainstay of Hawaiian music. Manufacturers of the steel guitar include: *Emmons, Sho-Bud, Fender, Weissenborn, Magnum, GFI* and many others. The only other instrument in the family to use the flat playing position is the bluegrass style *Dobro.*

Lute Guitar or Tenor Lute
The lute guitar is something of a hybrid instrument, combining characteristics of both the European lute and the guitar. The majority of models feature the traditional rounded ribbed back and teardrop body shape associated with the lute, but also retain the 6-string configuration and scale length of a guitar. The lute guitar's popularity has always been particularly high in Germany.

Octave, Soprano or Piccolo Guitar
As the name suggests, the octave guitar is tuned exactly an octave above standard tuning. The scale length is generally between 400-430mm (15¾ to 17 inches). Because of the very short scale, light strings need to be used.

Parlour Guitar
A small bodied style of acoustic guitar popular in the latter part of the 19th century up until the 1950s. The styling is a little like the size and shape of a baroque guitar.

Rajão
The 5-string rajão, like it's sister instrument, the braguinha, originates in the Portuguese island of Madeira where it's used mainly for rhythm accompaniment. The D-G-C-E-A tuning is re-entrant like the soprano ukulele, except it employs this configuration on both the 4th and 5th strings.

Re-entrant Tuning
Best exemplified by the aide-mémoire *"my dog has fleas"*, representing the 4 strings of the ukulele from 4th to 1st. A re-entrant arrangement refers to a tuning that doesn't follow a strict high to low or low to high succession. In the case of the soprano uke, the 3rd string is the lowest sounding, rather than 4th. The tenor and baritone models don't generally employ re-entrant tuning. The rajão, the predecessor to the uke, also features re-entrant tuning.

Requinto Guitar
The requinto is a shorter scaled version of the classical guitar pitched a 4th higher than standard E-A-D-G-B-E tuning. The A-D-G-C-E-A tuning can best be described as standard guitar tuning capoed at the 5th fret. Requintos feature prominently in Latin America, Mexico and Spain.

Semi-Acoustic Guitar
Running in parallel to the design of the solid-bodied electric, several leading companies including *Gibson, Gretsch* and *Rickenbacker* were developing popular lines of semi-acoustic models. These owe much of their ancestry to the earlier jazz archtops, with the use of hollow bodies and f-holes. Important models include the *Gibson 335* and *ES-175, Rickenbacker 300* and *400 Series* and the *Gretsch Country Gentleman* and *White Falcon.*

Soprano Ukulele
The origins of the ukulele began in 1879, when a German ship, the Ravenscrag, carried three cabinet makers, Manuel Nunes, Augusto Dias and Jose de Espirito Santo, to the Hawaiian islands to provide much needed cabinet making skills for the existing Madeiran emigrees. Although today we think of luthery and cabinet making as separate skills, it wasn't un-

common in previous centuries for a cabinet maker to double up his craft and maximize earnings by combining the two disciplines. So Nunes, possibly aided by Dias and Santo, came up with a design based on the body shape of the braguinha and the re-entrant tuning of the rajão, albeit with four strings instead of five.

The ukulele soon gained a foothold in Hawaiian life and culture, even finding its way into the hands of King David Kalaukea, a talented musician in his own right. Because the tuning was essentially a transposed four string guitar, people were immediately able to adjust to the new instrument. It wasn't long before this musical hybrid became a cultural icon and a tourist memento for anybody visiting the islands. Unlike other instruments whose popularity has waxed and waned over the years, the little uke has managed to stave off passing trends and remains a popular purchase for both young and old. According to historians, its greatest period of popularity lay between 1915-1935, when it became the number one musical instrument in the average American family home. It's unlikely since the emergence of the guitar in its many guises, that the little uke will rise to such dizzy heights again. But because of it's portability, relatively low starting price and ease of playing, it will always maintain a healthy niche position in the instrument market.

The name ukulele is officially thought to translate from the Hawaiian, as *jumping flea*. But another possible origin could lie in the words *ukeki*, a type of plucked Hawaiian jew's harp and *mele*, the local word for song.

Most quality instruments are generally constructed from the local koa wood, but you'll find makers using anything from plywood to cardboard to produce this little relative of the guitar. The tonal qualities of the latter, as you can imagine, are open to question!

Although we refer to the standard ukulele design today as the soprano, this prefix was added later to differentiate between the four family members. Standard tuning for most soprano ukes is GCEA (or an open C6 chord). ADF#B (open D6) was also used earlier in the 20th century for greater sound projection and is still popular with a minority of players today.

Seven-String Guitar
The original 7-string guitars were originally found in 19th century Russia and tuned to an open G major chord (D-G-B-D-G-B-D). These probably owe a little of their heritage to instruments such as the cittern and kobza. In Russia the 7-string is known as the *semistrunnaya gitara* or colloquially as the *semistrunka*.

The Brazilian incarnation of the 7-string is a popular instrument in *choro* and *samba* music where it's tuned to standard guitar tuning with an additional lower C in the bottom (C-E-A-D-G-B-E). The Brazilian playing technique of *baixaria* consists of counterpoint and accompaniment.

The Westernized 7-string is very similar to Brazilian tuning but instead of dropping down to a lower C, it descends half a tone to a B (B-E-A-D-G-B-E). In recent years the 7-string has become a popular niche instrument among rock guitarists such as Steve Vai. Jazz players also began experimenting with the extended instrument as early as the 1930s, where players such as George Van Eps tuned the 7th string down to a low A.

Sitar Guitar *or* Electric Sitar
The sitar guitar was invented in the late 1960s by American session player, Vincent Bell. To reproduce the familiar sitar sound, Bell designed a unique bridge system called the *buzz-bridge*. This innovative feature was installed in Danelectro's first production model called the *Coral Electric Sitar*, which also featured 13 sympathetic drone strings. The electric sitar guitar has been utilized to great effect over the years by many leading musicians including: Jimmy Page, Steve Howe and Jeff Beck.

Portuguese Guitar *or* Portuguese Guitarra
The guitarra is a 12-string double course instrument used almost exclusively in Portuguese *Fado* music. There are two distinct designs with their own traditional regional tunings. Firstly, the Coimbra with its teardrop headstock protuberance and 470-490mm scale length tuned C-G-A-D-G-A. Secondly, the Lisboa or Lisbon guitarra, features a violin-like scroll on the headstock and a shorter scale length of 440 or 458mm. The instrument is pitched D-A-B♭-E-A-B and is particularly associated with the accompaniment of *Fado* singing. Both forms feature octave strings on the lowest three courses. Stylistically, the guitarra seems more at home among the mandolin/cittern family of instruments, than as a true form of the guitar.

Taropatch
The taropatch is an 8-string variant of the ukulele divided up into 4 double courses. Its origins lie with the rajão after native Hawaiians adopted the ukulele, but wanted a bigger overall sound. An additional course was added to each string and the result was the taropatch *'fiddle'* as it came to be known.

Tenor Guitar
The original 4-string tenor guitars were produced with the tenor banjo player in mind. Often a guitar sound was needed, but this meant the banjo player having to master a completely new instrument. So, the basic tuning and scale length of the tenor were retained, with a guitar body replacing the circular head and body of the banjo. The standard C-G-D-A tuning of the tenor is traditionally based on the tenor jazz banjo, but today the popular Irish tuning of G-D-A-E has also gained wide spread acceptance. Both tunings are featured in this guide.

Leading manufacturers over the years have included: *Gibson, C.F. Martin & Co, Epiphone, Regal, Gretsch, Harmony, National, Guild and Stella*. Today they're a lot trickier to locate, but the likes of *Gibson* and *Martin* still produce commercial models and a few specialist independent luthiers build tenors as one of their stock designs. Major tenor guitar luthiers include: David Hodson, Shelley Park, Joel Eckhaus (*Earnest Instruments*) and Steve Parks.

Tenor Ukulele
The second largest of the ukulele family. The tenor differs from the soprano and concert models in its use of the optional guitar-style high to low stringing, rather than the re-entrant configuration found on traditional ukes. The tenor also uses re-entrant tuning. The most popular tuning for the tenor is identical to the soprano and concert models, G-C-E-A, but D-G-B-E has also gained favour with many musicians over the years, including famous uke players like Lyle Ritz.

Terz *or* Tierce Guitar
The terz is a form of classical guitar tuned up to G instead of standard E-string tuning. It was particularly popular in 19th century Vienna.

Timple
A close relative of the ukulele originating in the Canary Islands and Murcia, the timple (pronounced *teem-play*) has an additional fifth string and a distinctive rounded back. The tuning is generally A-D-F#-B-E (from low to high). Basically, a traditional ukulele D6 tuning with an additional high E string. 4-string versions also exist. The timple is thought to have Berber origins.

Tiple
Unlike its Hawaiian relative, the tiple in its many incarnations, is generally strung with steel strings which are arranged in triple and double courses. The version familiar to American and Western musicians was designed by *C.F. Martin & Company*, better known for their prowess in acoustic

guitar design. The *Martin* tiple is usually tuned A-D-F#-B with the middle two courses tripled and the two outer courses doubled.

Other types of tiple include:
Banjo Tiple (Peru): *A little banjo with 4 double courses of strings.*
Colombian Tiple: *12-string guitar-like instrument divided up into 4 triple stringed courses*
Marxochime Hawaiian Tiple: *A zither-lap steel guitar hybrid tiple.*
Spanish Tiple (Spain): *A little guitar style tiple from Menorca.*
Tiple Argentino (Argentina): *Little guitar-style instrument with 6 strings.*
Tiple Cubano (Cuba): *Cuban instrument with either 5 single string or 5 double courses (like the taropatch or charango).*
Tiple Doliente (Puerto Rico): *A popular five stringed instrument.*
Tiple Dominicano (Dominican Republic): *5 double coursed bandurria-like instrument*
Tiple Grande de Ponce (Puerto Rico): *A narrow waisted, larger member of the tiple group.*
Tiple Peruano (Peru): *Peruvian tiple with 4 single or double strings.*
Tiple Requinto Costanero (Puerto Rico): *Small version of the tiplón.*
Tiple Requinto de la Montaña (Puerto Rico): *Small 3-stringed version of the doliente.*
Tiple Uruguayo (Uruguay): *A little guitar-style of tiple with 6 strings.*
Tiple Venezolano (Venezuela): *Smaller version of the Colombian tiple, featuring 4 triple string courses.*
Tiplón *or* Tiple con Macho (Puerto Rico): *The largest family member with a 5th tuning peg much like the 5-string banjo.*

The word *tiple* (pronounced *tee-play*) translated from the Spanish, means treble or soprano.

Twelve-String Guitar
The origin of the 12-string is a little blurred to say the least. The first theory goes back to the beginning of the 20th century where Italian luthiers working for guitar companies such as *Harmony, Oscar Schmidt* and *Regal* used their knowledge of double course instruments such as the mandolin to adapt their designs to suit the bigger instrument. The second theory involves the adaptation of varying Mexican or South American instruments such as the cuatro, tiple, charango or bajo sexto. This second theory seems equally viable as these fretted cousins of the guitar also feature courses of double metal strings (apart from the charango which originally used gut - replaced today by nylon or composite materials). Because of the immense strain placed on the neck by the strings, the 12-string is sometimes tuned down below standard guitar tuning to prevent warping, and capoed at an appropriate fret. The stringing arrangement features unison pairs on the first two courses, followed by either a unison pair or octaves on the third and octaves again on the fourth, fifth and sixth.

Apart from the ever popular acoustic models that have sprung up over the years, the 12-string has also found its niche in the electric ranks. The most successful models probably being the *Rickenbacker 360* (so beloved of artists like *The Byrd's* Roger McGuinn) and Gibson's 6/12 double-neck SG, the *EDS-1275*.

Ukelele
Alternative spelling of ukulele.

Ukulele-Banjo, Banjo-Ukulele *or* Banjolele
A popular instrument with its heyday in the 20's and 30's, the banjolele or banjo-uke is basically a ukulele in a short scaled banjo's body. These entertaining instruments can be tuned GCEA or ADF#B. The banjolele was popularized in the U.K. by comedian *George Formby*, where the instrument was mistakenly referred to at the time as a ukulele. The name banjolele was originally created by the *Keech Brothers, Alvin* and *Kel*.

Vihuela
The vihuela or 5-stringed Mexican guitar employs a body shape very much akin to its large relative, the guitarrón. It's mainly considered to be a rhythm or accompanying instrument played with the fingers. Like the lute, the frets are normally tied on rather than fixed, with a standard tuning of A-D-G-B-E.

Venezuelan Cuatro
The South American cuatro's history can be traced back to its long defunct ancestor, the 4-string Spanish guitar. Again, like several of the instruments in this family group, the cuatro is tuned to the same fundamental intervals as the first four strings of a classical guitar - in this case A-D-F#-B, like the soprano uke's D6 tuning. Where it differs is in the positioning of the re-entrant strings. With the ukulele and rajão, the higher strings can be found on the 4th and 5th strings. With the cuatro, the 2nd and 3rd strings are re-entrant (namely the D and F#). Although most musicians use this tuning, an alternative was created by reknowned cuatro player, Fredy Reyna in 1948. Rebelling against the re-entrant standard, Reyna re-strung the cuatro to a more recognizable low to high tuning (E-A-C#-F#), but still retained the relationship, based on guitar tuning (transposed into the key of A6).

Very much akin to the English language aide-mémoire *"my dog has fleas"*, the cuatro's tuning can be remembered by singing the following two words, *"Cam-bur pin-tón"*, or ripe banana!

The 4-string or Venezuelan cuatro is not to be confused with the Puerto Rican cuatro which illogically has 10 steel strings in 5 double courses. The design bares little or no resemblance to the more guitar-like mainland instrument (the tuning is B-E-A-D-G). The shape is very reminiscent of a member of the violin family with it's instantly recognizable sculpted waist and upper/lower bouts.

UKULELE TUNINGS

The following list of ukulele family tunings includes the regular members of the uke family as well as a selection of their more exotic cousins. Also included is the guitalele, although it could equally have a foot in the guitar family camp.

Ukulele Family Instrument Tunings

Akulele	DGBE (G6)
Baritone Ukulele Standard Tuning	DGBE (G6)
Concert Ukulele Standard Tuning	GCEA (C6)
Concert Ukulele Alternative Tuning	ADF♯B (D6)
Soprano Akulele Standard Tuning	GCEA (C6)
Soprano Ukulele Standard Tuning	GCEA (C6)
Soprano Ukulele Alternative Tuning	ADF♯B (D6)
Sopranino Akulele Standard Tuning	DGBE (G6)
Taropatch Standard Tuning	GCEA (C6)
Tenor Ukulele Standard Tuning	GCEA (C6)
Tenor Ukulele Alternative Tuning	DGBE (G6)
Ukulele-Banjo Standard Tuning	GCEA (C6)
Ukulele-Banjo Alternative Tuning	ADF♯B (D6)

Related Instrument Tunings

Braguinha Standard Tuning	DGBD (G Major)
Cavaquinho Standard Tuning	DGBD (G Major)
Cavaquinho Alternative tuning	GGBD (G Major)
Cavaquinho Alternative Tuning	AAC♯E (A Major)
Cavaquinho Guitar Tuning	DGBE (G6)
Charango Standard Tuning	GCEAE (C6)
Charangon Standard Tuning 1	CFADA (F6)
Charangon Standard Tuning 2	DGBEB (G6)
Guitalele Standard Tuning	ADGCEA
Martin Tiple Standard Tuning	ADF♯B (D6)
Rajão Standard Tuning	DGCEA (C6/9)
Ronroco Standard Tuning	GCEAE (G6)
Timple Canario Standard Tuning	ADF♯BE (D6/9)
Tiple (American)	ADF♯B (D6)
Tiple (Colombian Modern)	DBGE (G6)
Tiple (Colombian Traditional)	CEAD
Venezuelan Cuatro Standard Tuning	ADF♯B (D6)
Venezuelan Cuatro F. Reyna Tuning	EAC♯F♯ (A6)
Walaycho Standard Tuning 1	CFADA (F6)
Walaycho Standard Tuning 2	DGBEB (G6)

GUITAR TUNINGS

The following list of guitar tunings includes a selection of some popular standards as well as some personal favourites. Some players stick with the same two ot three tunings all their lives, but others enjoy experimenting with new set-ups, but whichever you decide to do, have fun with this versatile family of instruments!

6-String Guitar

Drop D	DADGBE
Double Drop D	DADGBD
Dadgad or Dsus4	DADGAD
Lute & Vihuela Tuning	EADF♯BE
Open C	CGCGCE
Open D	DADF♯AD
Open E	EBEG♯BE
Open Em	EBEGBE
Open G	DGDGBD
Open Gm	DGDGB♭D
Open A	EAEAC♯E
Rev. Gary Davis Bottleneck Tuning	DADF♯AB
Skip James Open Em Tuning	EBEGBE
Standard Tuning	EADGBE

7-String Guitar

Brazilian Tuning	CEADGBE
Jazz Tuning	AEADGBE
Standard & Brazilian Alternate Tuning	BEADGBE
Russian Tuning	DGBDGBD

10-String Guitar

Modern or Yepes Tuning	G♭A♭B♭CEADGBE

12-String Guitar

Standard Tuning	EADGBE

Baritone Guitar

Standard 4th Below Guitar Tuning	BEADF♯B
Standard 5th Below Guitar Tuning	ADGCEA
Octave (lower) Tuning	EADGBE

Bass Guitar

Standard 4-String Tuning	EADG
Standard 5-String B Tuning	BEADG
Standard 5-String C Tuning	EADGC
Standard 6-String Tuning	BEADGC
Standard 7-String Tuning	BEADGCF
Standard 8-String Tuning	F♯BEADGCF

Dobro

Standard Tuning	GBDGBD

Tenor Guitar

Standard Tuning	CGDA
Irish	GDAE
Chicago	DGBE

Others

Bajo Quinto 10-String Tuning	ADGCF
Bajo Sexto 12-String Tuning	EADGCF
Bajo Sexto 12-String Mexican Tuning	EADGBE
Baroque Guitar Standard Tuning	ADGBE
English Guittar Standard Tuning	CEGCEG
Guitarrón Standard Tuning	ADGBE
Octave Guitar Standard Octave Tuning	EADGBE
Portuguese Guitarra Coimbra Tuning	CGADGA
Portuguese Guitarra Lisboa Tuning	DAB♭EAB
Requinto Standard Tuning	ADGCEA
Terz Guitar Standard Tuning	GCFA♯DG
Vihuela Standard Tuning	ADGBE

ALTERNATIVE CHORD NAMES

C	**CM or Cmaj**
Cm	**Cmin or C-**
C-5	**C-5 or C(♭5)**
C°	**Cdim**
C4	**Csus4(no 5th) or Csus(no 5th)**
C5	**C Power Chord or C(no 3rd)**
Csus2	**C(sus2) or C2**
Csus4	**Csus or C(sus4)**
Csus4add9	**Csus(add9)**
C+	**Caug, C+5 or C(♯5)**
C6	**CM6 or CMaj6**
Cadd9	**Cadd2**
Cm6	**C-6 or Cmin6**
Cmadd9	**Cmadd2 or C-(add9)**
C6add9	**C6/9, C⁶₉ or CMaj6(add9)**
Cm6add9	**Cm6/9 or Cm⁶₉**
C°7	**Cdim7**
C7	**Cdom**
C7sus2	**C7(sus2)**
C7sus4	**C7sus, C7(sus4) or Csus11**
C7-5	**C7♭5**
C7+5	**C7+ or C7♯5**
C7-9	**C7♭9 or C7(add♭9)**
C7+9	**C7♯9 or C7(add♯9)**
C7-5-9	**C7♭5♭9**
C7+5-9	**C7♯5♭9**
C7+5+9	**C7♯5♯9**
C7add11	**C7/11 or C₁₁⁷**
C7+11	**C7♯11**
Cm7	**C-7, Cmi7 or Cmin7**
Cm7-5	**Cm7♭5, C-7-5 or C°̸**
Cm7-5-9	**Cm7♭5♭9**
Cm7-9	**Cm7♭9**
Cm7add11	**Cm**
Cm(maj7)	**Cm♯7, CM7-5, CmM7 or C-△**
Cmaj7	**CM7 or C△(Delta)**
Cmaj7-5	**CM7-5, C△♭5 or Cmaj7♭5**
Cmaj7+5	**CM7+5, C△5+ or Cmaj7♯11**
Cmaj7+11	**CM7+11, C△+♯11 or Cmaj7♯11**
C9	**C7(add9)**
C9sus4	**C9sus or C9(sus4)**
C9-5	**C9♭5**
C9+5	**C9♯5**
C9+11	**C9♯11**
Cm9	**C-9 or Cmin9**
Cm9-5	**Cm9♭5**
Cm(maj9)	**Cm9(maj7), CmM9 or Cm(addM9)**
Cmaj9	**CM9, Cmaj7(add9), C△9 or CM7(add9)**
Cmaj9-5	**CM9-5, Cmaj9♭5, C△9♭5 or CM9♭5**
Cmaj9+5	**CM9+5, Cmaj9♯5, C△9♯5**
Cmaj9add6	**CM9add6 or C△9add6**
Cmaj9+11	**CM9+11, Cmaj9♯11, C△9♯11 or CM9♯11**
C11	**C7(add11)**
C11-9	**C11♭9**
Cm11	**C-11 or Cmin11**
Cmaj11	**CM11, Cmaj7(add11), C△11, CM7(add11)**
C13	**C7/6(no 9th) or C7(add13)**
C13sus4	**C13sus or C13(sus4)**
C13-5-9	**C13♭5♭9**
C13-9	**C13♭9**
C13+9	**C13♯9**
C13+11	**C13♯11 or C13aug11**

Cm13	**C-13 or Cmin13**
Cmaj13	**CM13, Cmaj7(add13), C△13 or CM7(add13)**

M	major
m	minor
-	minor
dim	diminished
°	diminished
ø	half diminished
sus	suspended
aug	augmented
+	augmented
add	added
dom	dominant
△	delta /major seventh
Q(3)	quartal / double fourth
♯	sharp
×	double sharp
♭	flat
♭♭	double flat

Do	Spanish for C
Dó	Portuguese for C
Re	Spanish for D
Ré	Portuguese for D
Mi	Spanish & Portuguese for E
Fa	Spanish & Portuguese for F
So	Spanish for G
Sol	Portuguese for G
La	Spanish for A
Lá	Portuguese for A
Si	Spanish & Portuguese for B
H	German for B

English Tonic Sol-fa

Do	**C**
Re	**D**
Me	**E**
Fa	**F**
Sol	**G**
La	**A**
Ti	**B**

The majority of music books will use the chords featured in the first column (on the far left and top right), but should you come across alternatives, consult this guide for other naming conventions.

The list above includes most of the symbols and abbreviations that you're likely to encounter in the majority of music books.

NOTES

NOTES

NOTES

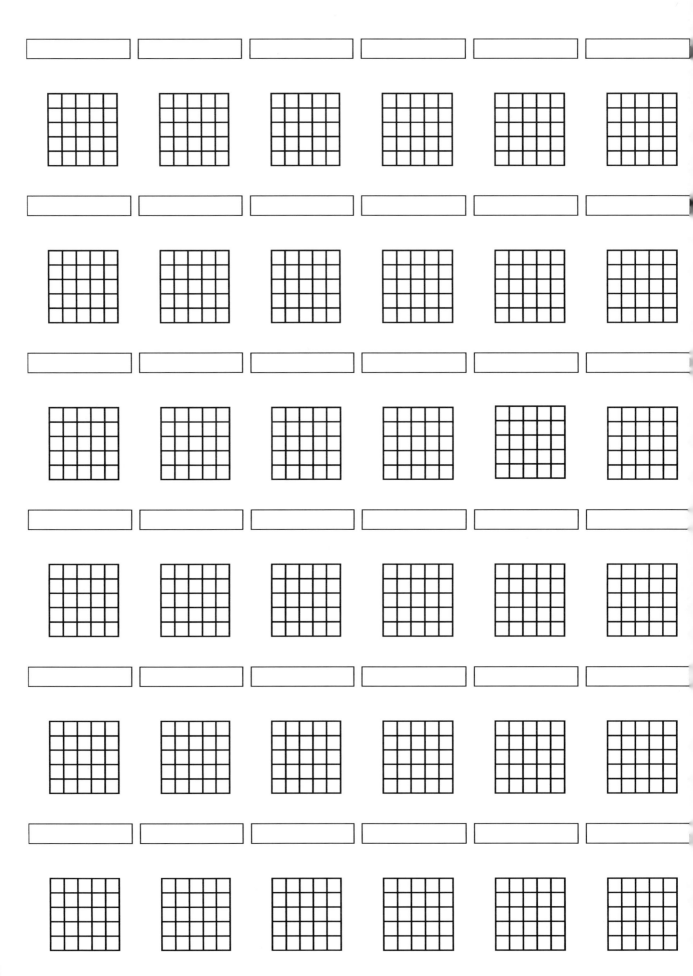

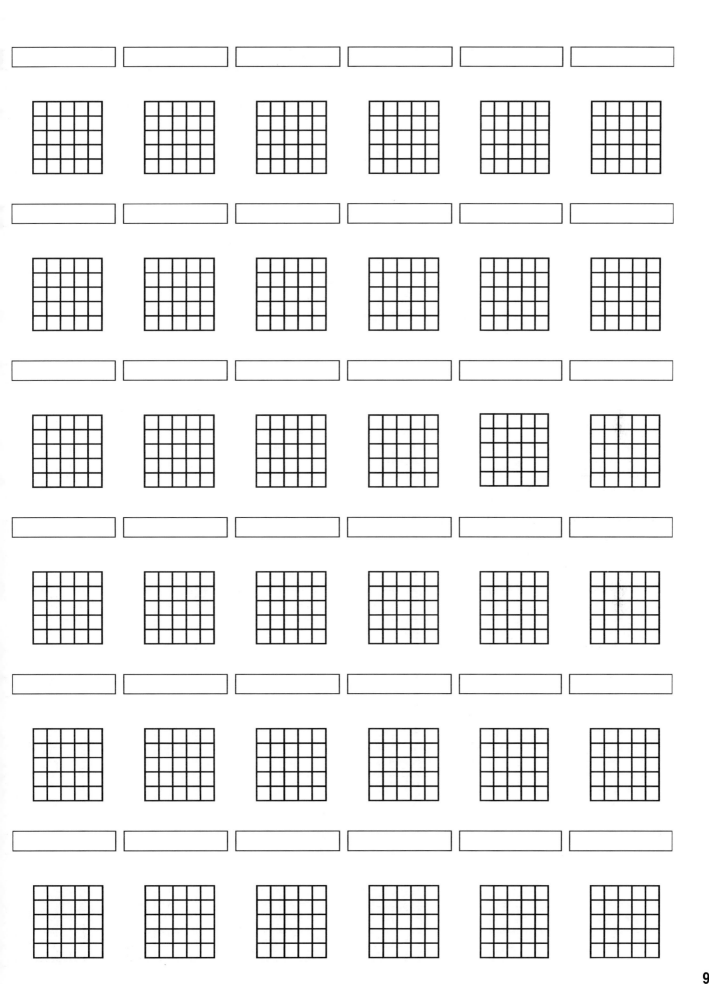

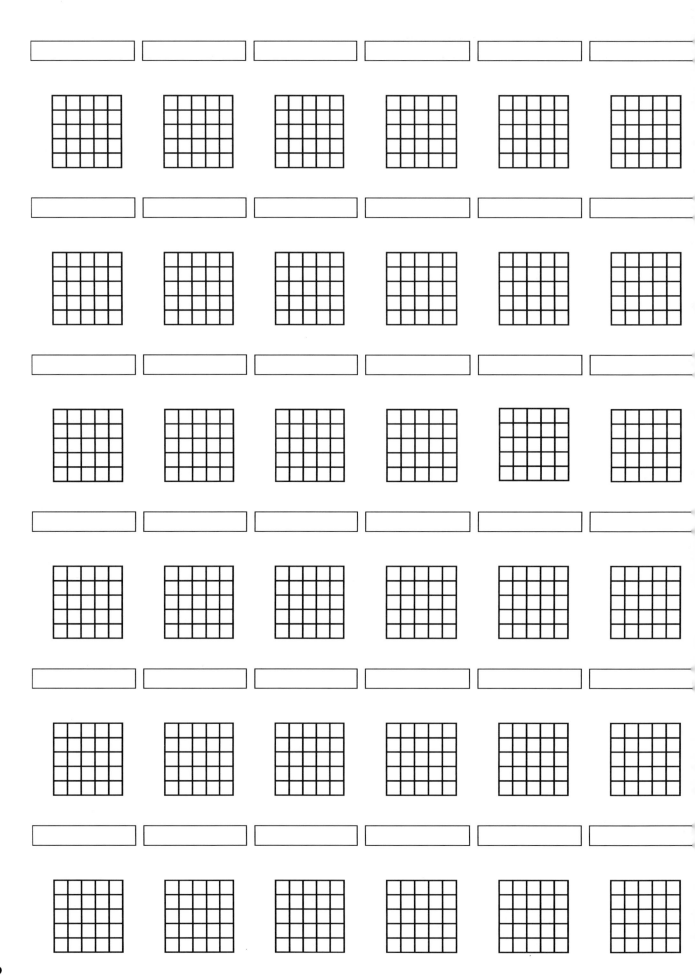

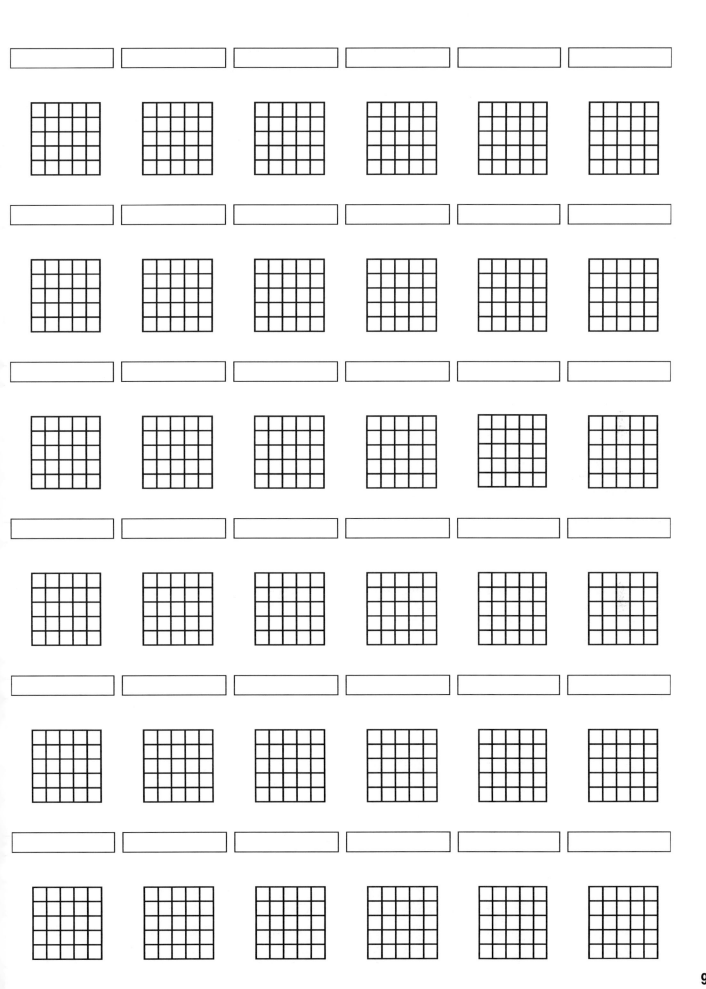

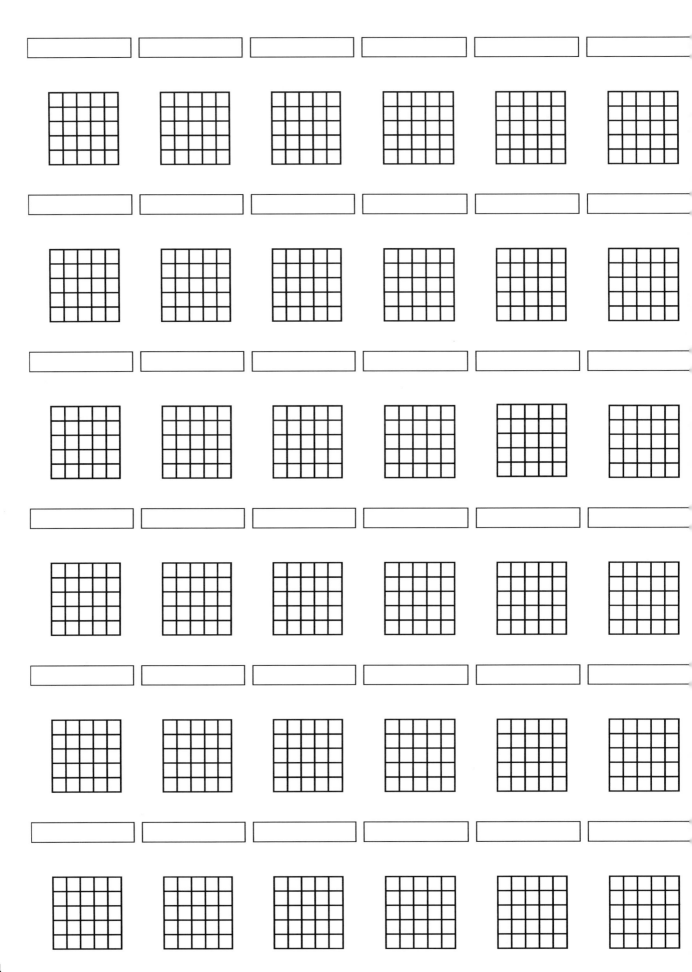

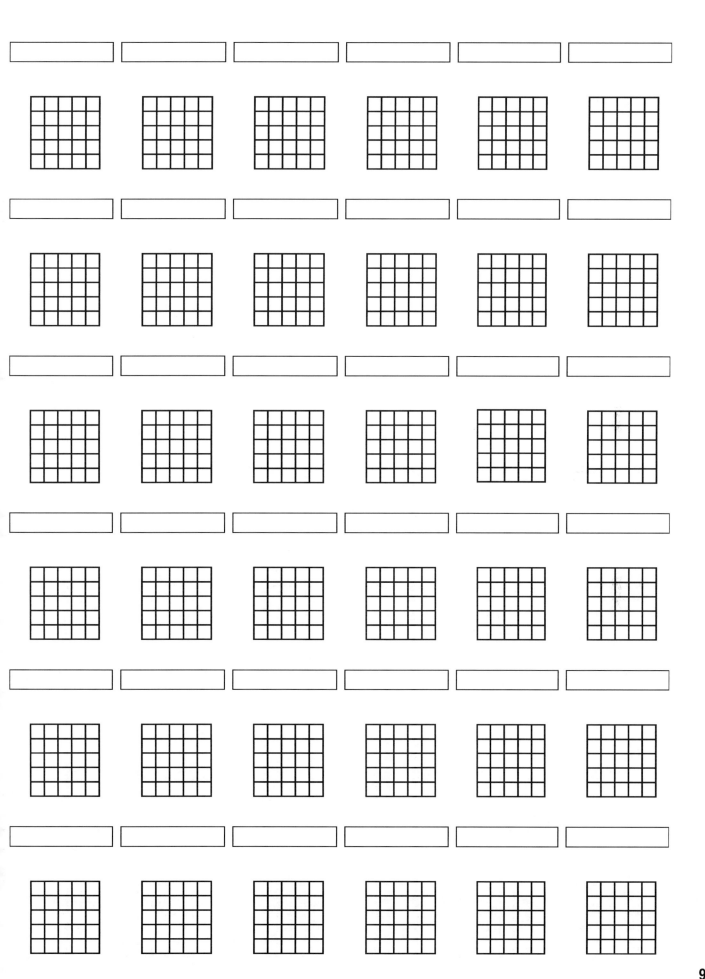

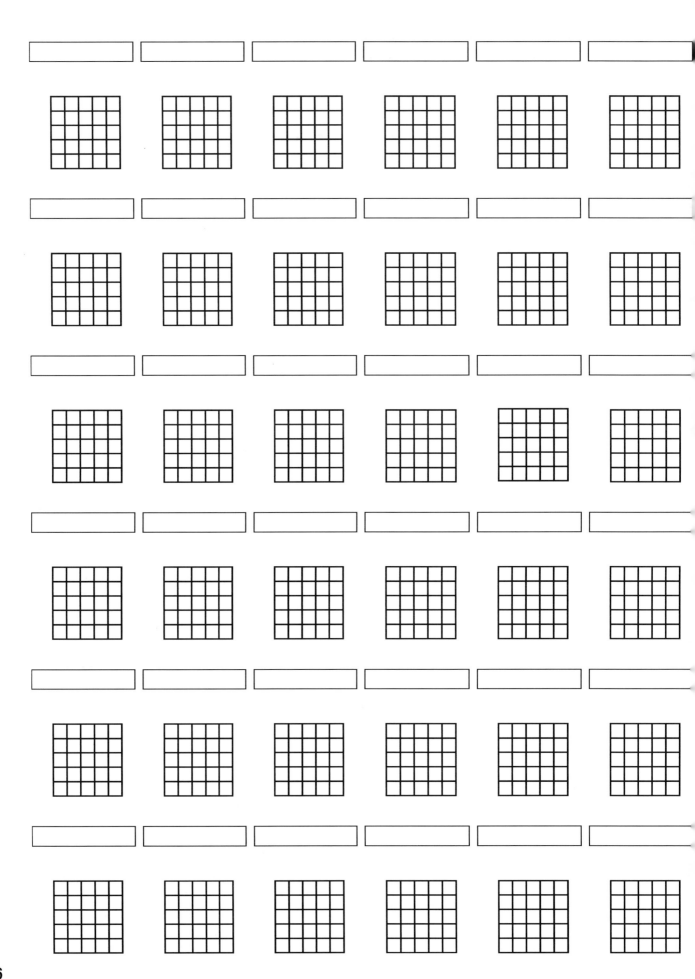

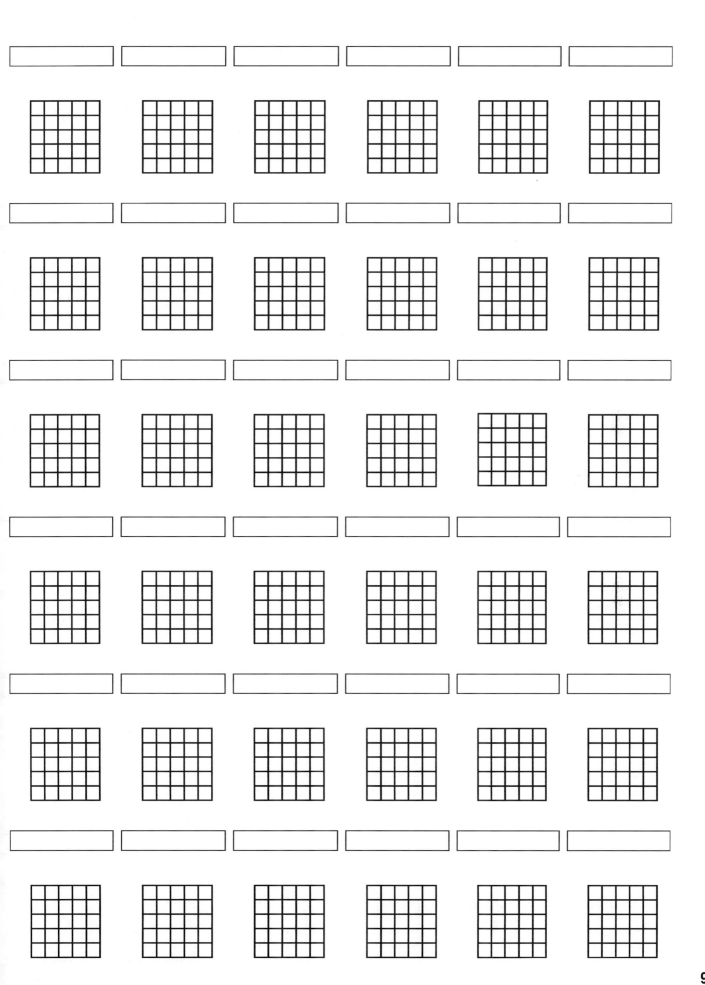

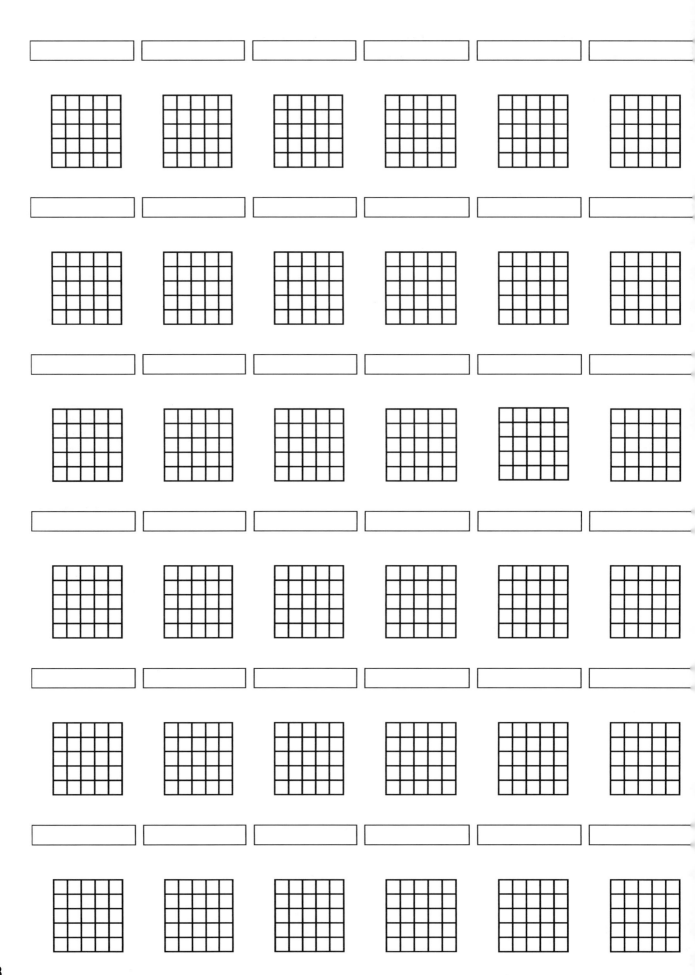

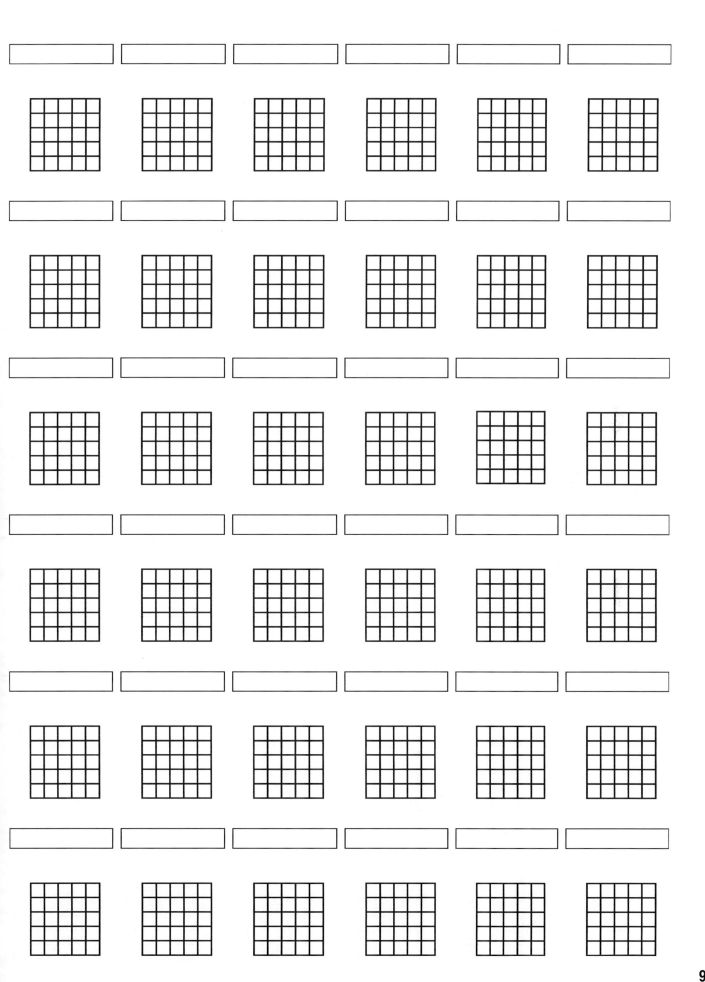

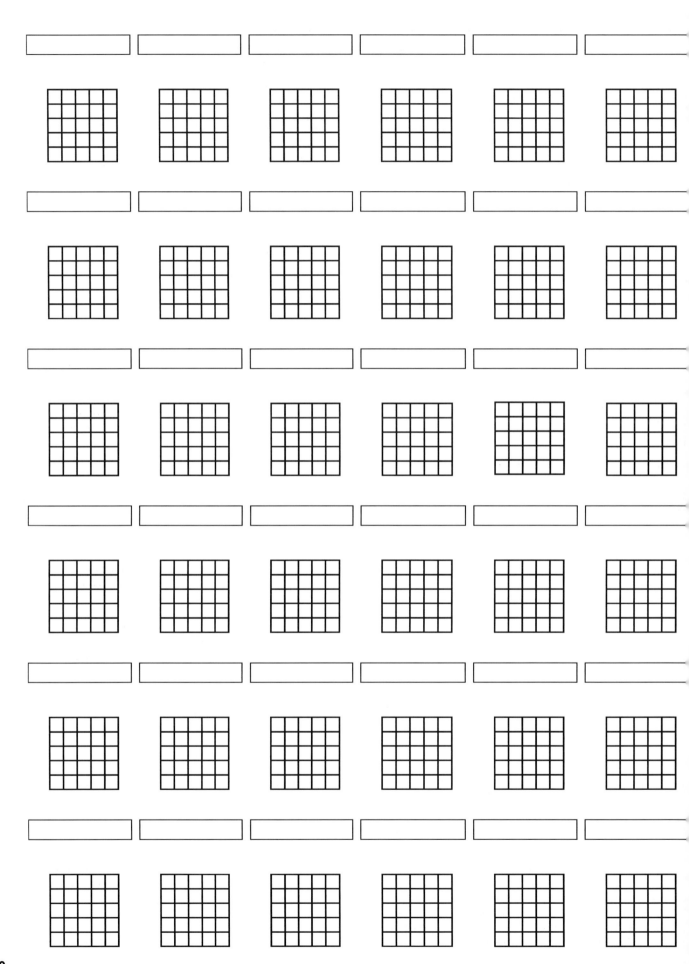

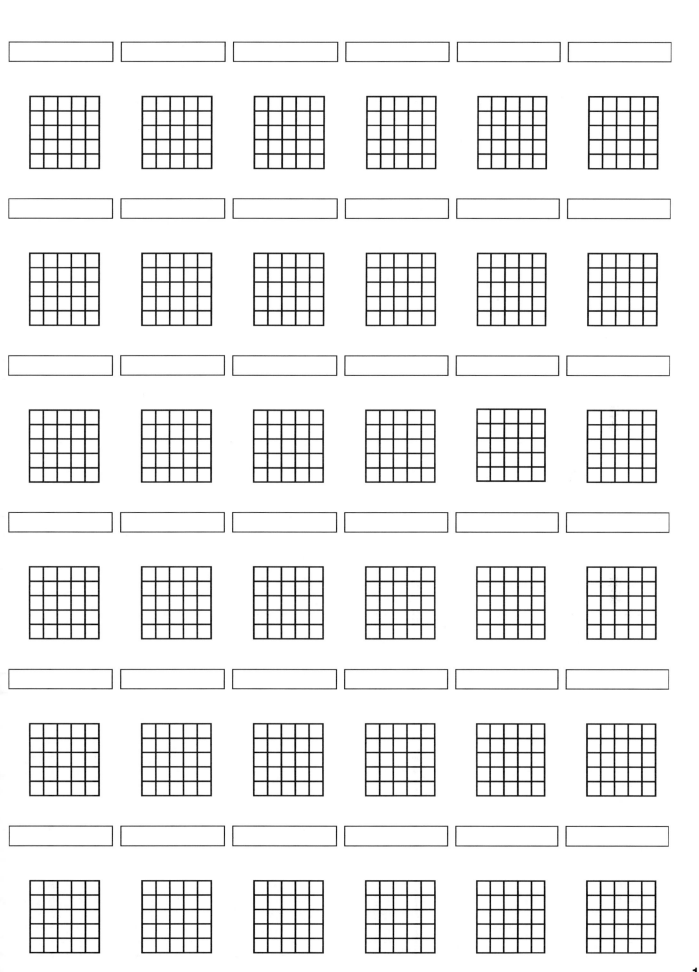

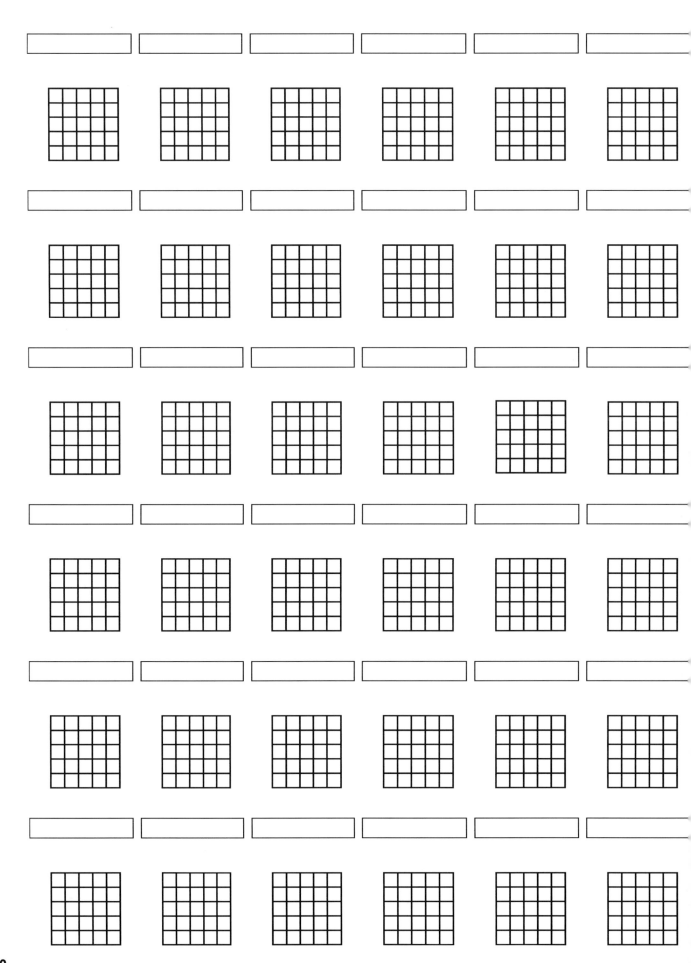

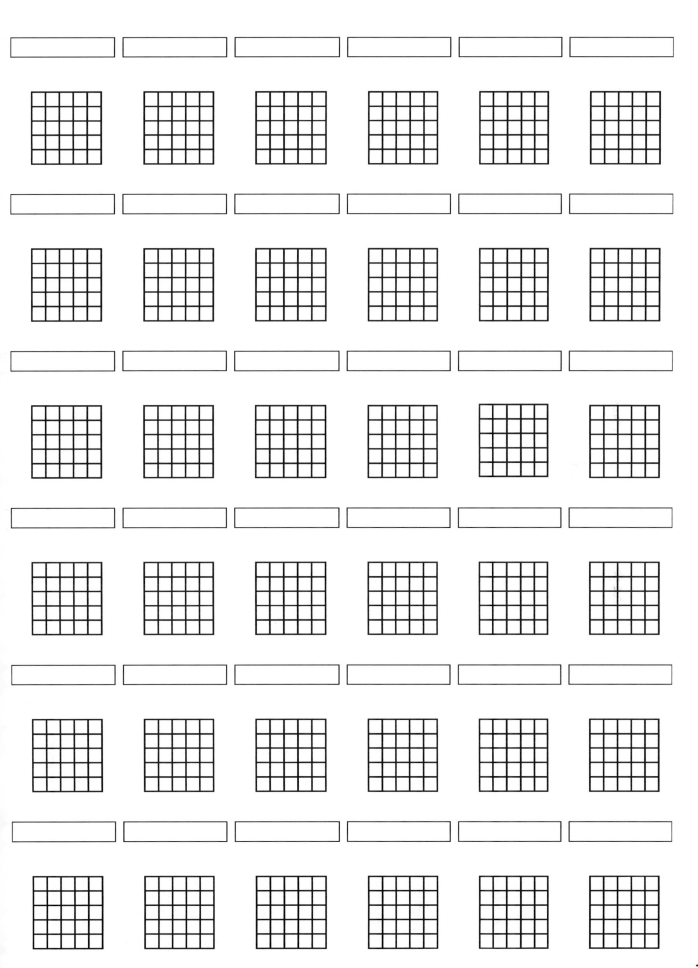

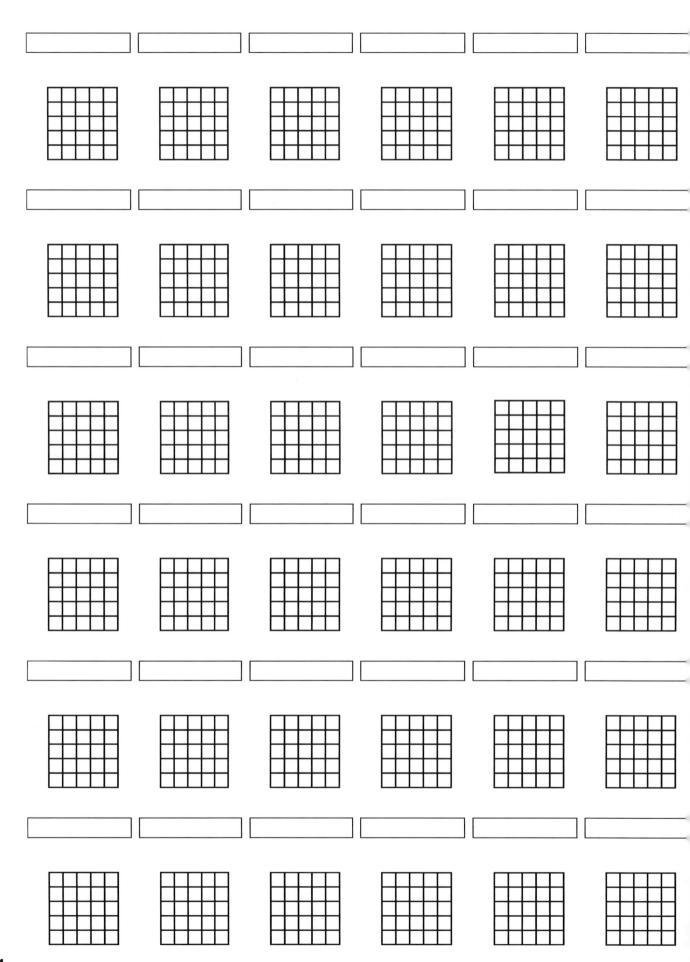

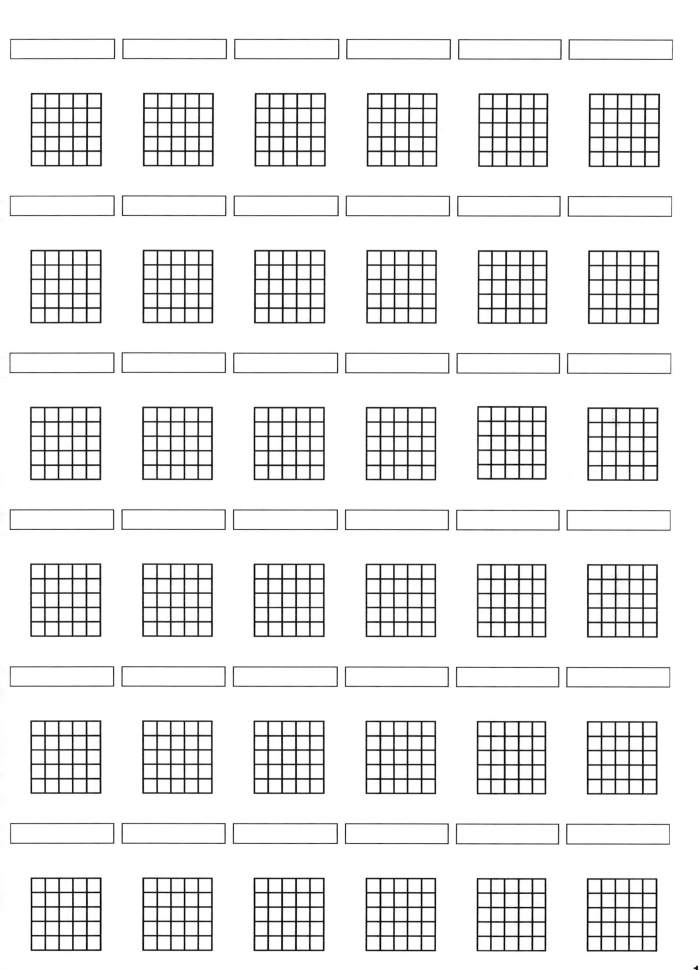

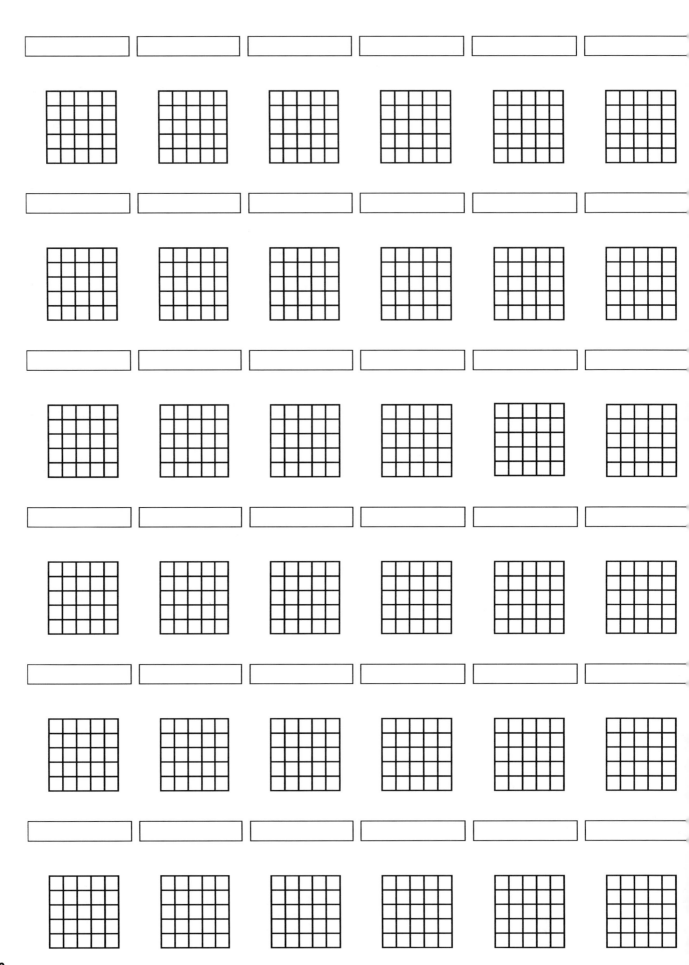

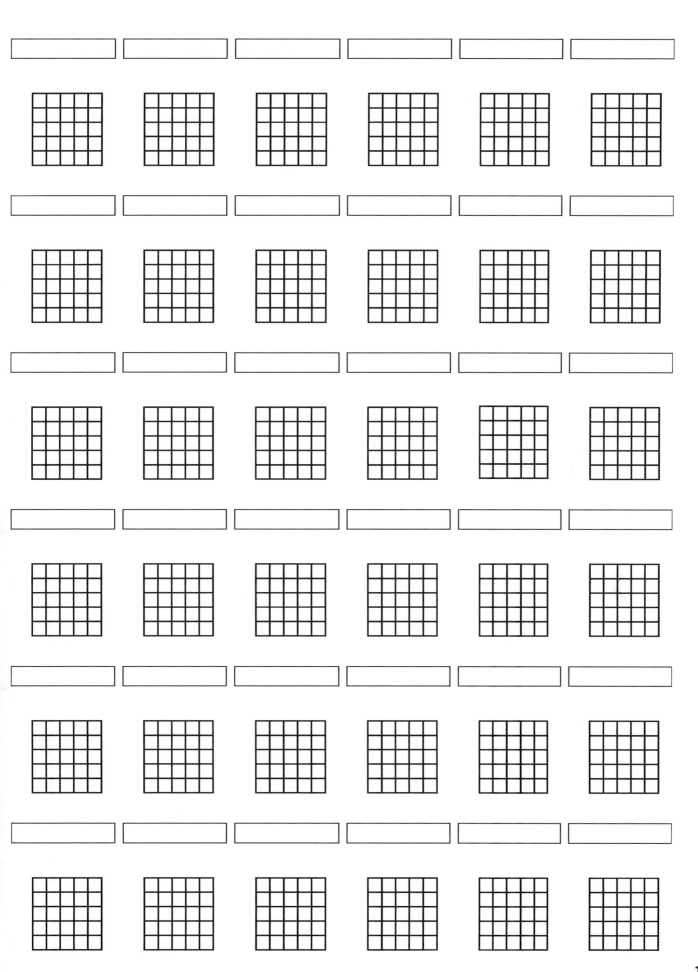

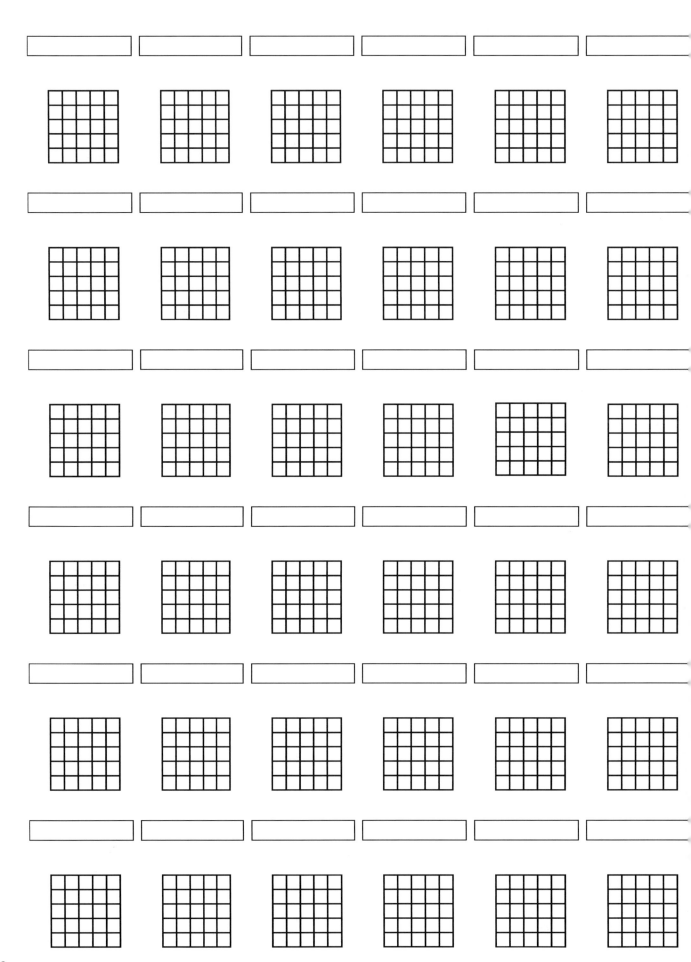

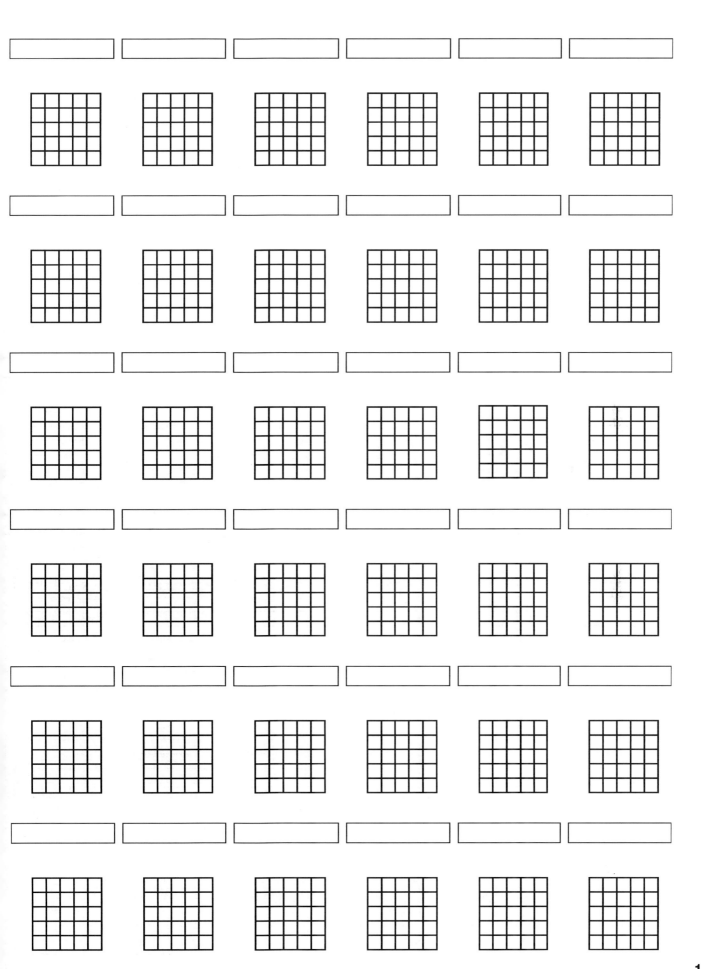

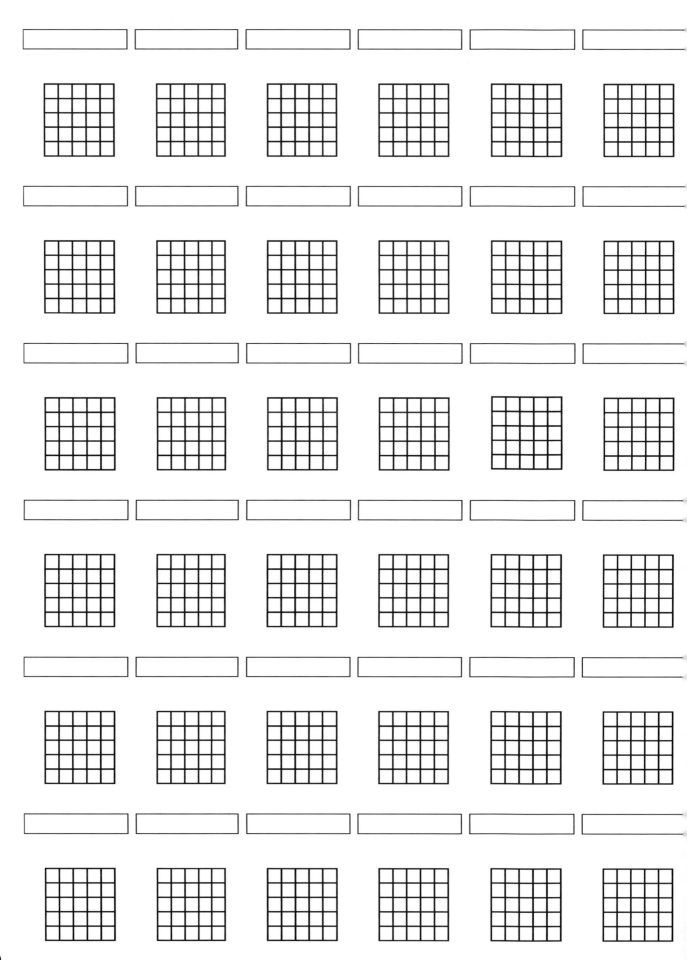

12939125R00062

Made in the USA
San Bernardino, CA
12 December 2018